paper pom-poms

party

and other

decorations

paper pom-poms

party and other decorations

35 step-by-step projects
to make with tissue,
paper, and card

Juliet Carr

CICO BOOKS
LONDON NEW YORK

For my mother, Maggie Carr

Published in 2015 by CICO Books
An imprint of Ryland Peters & Small Ltd
20–21 Jockey's Fields   341 E 116th St
London WC1R 4BW   New York, NY 10029

www.rylandpeters.com

10 9 8 7 6 5 4 3 2 1

A CIP catalog record for this book is available from the
Library of Congress and the British Library.

ISBN: 978 1 78249 243 6

Printed in China

Editor: Clare Sayer
Designer: Louise Leffler
Photographers: Holly Jolliffe and Emma Mitchell
Template illustrator: Stephen Dew
Stylists: Juliet Carr, Nel Haynes, and Luis Peral

Senior editor: Carmel Edmonds
In-house designer: Fahema Khanam
Art director: Sally Powell
Production controller: Sarah Kulasek-Boyd
Publishing manager: Penny Craig
Publisher: Cindy Richards

contents

introduction

I was always a creative, arty type at school and university, but over the course of my career in interior design and project management, I had never been able to set aside the time to create any artworks or handcrafted items—although the wish to do so had always been there. So five years ago, I left my day job and started my company, Paperpoms UK, and now I get to make and invent new paper flowers and decorations all day long! From paper flower bouquets for the Queen and paperpoms for Madonna, to giant paper roses for window displays, every item is lovingly handmade.

I didn't think I would ever be writing the introduction to a book, let alone a book that I'd created about my greatest passion: decorative papercraft.

The wonderful thing about paper is that it is so versatile, whether it is the lightest tissue paper or a rigid corrugated card, and we've chosen to include projects that take advantage of the various qualities of different types of paper. Some of the 35 projects in the book can be made with papers or materials that might have been stashed away in drawers or boxes because they were pretty or too nicc to throw out. I always kccp giftwrap, greeting cards, old calendars, and paper, ephemera with interesting patterns or prints on them, in the hope that I'll be able to use them again and in a creative way.

Within the pages of this book I will show you how to make the ever-versatile paper pom-pom (I call them poms!), as well as paper flowers, garlands, wreaths, and table centerpieces, all made using basic crafting tools and easy techniques. It is amazing what you can create with paper, scissors, ribbon, and glue! With a few simple twists, folds, nips, and tucks, it is easy to transform a flat, humble piece of paper into a beautiful, modern decoration that will have pride of place in any party or room. This unique book is full of creative tips and advice, with step-by-step photographs that show simple and effective techniques for each of the projects.

If you are planning a wedding, a baby shower, or a party for any occasion, you are sure to find a stunning selection of projects that you could choose to make. Combine tassel garlands with paper poms to decorate seemingly vast marquees, and entwine leaf garlands around banisters or church pews. Surprise your loved ones with giant crepe paper roses and hearts. Get a group of your friends and family together to make big batches of the projects at hen parties for weddings, as a gift for a mum-to-be—or just for fun! Or sit quietly by yourself and enjoy the satisfaction of learning a new skill and taking pride in creating something you have never made before—you never know what it might inspire you to make next or where it may lead...

materials and tools

The beauty of paper poms is that you can get started with just a few materials and I've designed most of the projects in this book so that they can be made with readily available materials, many of which you may already have in your craft box at home. It's a good idea to build up a supply of tissue and crepe paper, but I also keep giftwrap, pretty magazine pages, newspaper, catalogs and flyers that arrive in the mail, and old books, in the hope that I'll find a use for them. I usually do! Other everyday items like plain printer paper, coffee filters, and paper cupcake cases make an appearance, so keep an eye out for them too, as well as ribbon, string, pretty masking tape, and garden wires. See page 127 for a full list of stockists.

Papers

The projects in this book use a variety of different paper types, from delicate tissue paper to heavy cardstock and corrugated card from packaging boxes. Paper density is measured in grams per square meter (gsm), and some of the projects may specify a particular gsm in order to achieve the best results.

Tissue paper

Tissue paper sheets come in many colors and sizes and can either be machine finished (MF) or machine glazed (MG). Machine-finished papers are normally around 17gsm and are very crisp and translucent, while machine-glazed tissue is slightly denser (around 18gsm) and is shiny on one side and matte on the other. Very thin tissue can tear easily when you are working with it, so bear this in mind—I have found that the 17gsm MG tissue paper, which is 18 x 28in (45 x 70cm), tends to be very, very thin—so much so that it tears very easily when worked with—so we use the slightly larger sheets of machine-glazed tissue for most of our projects, both in the studio and for the projects in this book. A good size to work with is 20 x 30in (50 x 75cm).

Crepe paper

Crepe paper is made from a type of tissue paper that is coated with a glue-like substance and then creased (or "creped") to create a coarser and slightly heavier paper. Crepe paper also comes in a variety of weights. We often use doublette crepe paper, which has a different color on each side, making it an ideal choice for two-tone flowers or other poms. Crepe papers also have differing amounts of elasticity in

them, which can give them a double, triple, or quadruple stretch. We used Italian quadruple-stretch crepe paper for the Giant Rose on page 87 and double-stretch crepe paper for the Leaves on Twine on page 48. Crepe paper is sold either as folded sheets or on a roll. Standard rolls are usually 2¾yd (2.5m) long and 20in (50cm) wide. You can also find rolls of crepe paper streamers—we used these for the Paper Wisteria on page 112.

Other papers

Plain printer paper is widely availably in a range of colors and weights, from 80gsm to 300gsm, which is basically a cardstock. We used a 200gsm paper for projects like the Rosette Snowflakes (page 18) and 3-D Star Mobile (page 39). Look for patterned or metallic paper and card, and always keep card from cereal boxes or packaging. A great source of corrugated card is delivery boxes, or ask at your local supermarket.

Above: 1 rolled crepe paper **2** folded crepe paper **3** metallic foil (Mylar) **4** colored and glittered cardstock **5** crepe paper streamers **6** tissue paper **7** giftwrap and origami paper

Don't be scared to try out different materials and experiment with textures—doing this will make your projects very unique. Plain paper or cardstock can be decorated with pretty tapes or painted—just bear in mind that you don't want to use too much wet paint or your paper will become soggy!

Above: 1 green garden/florist's wire **2** monofilament/fishing line **3** polystyrene cups **4** food coloring **5** parcel tape **6** star hole punch **7** paper-covered wire (bind wire) **8** twine **9** mini brads (paper fasteners) and grommets (eyelets) **10** washi tape **11** masking tape **12** modeling clay **13** pink ribbon **14** baker's twine **15** paper scissors **16** fancy-edge scissors **17** craft knife **18** rotary cutter **19** florist's tape **20** paintbrush and container **21** white ribbon **22** clothespins **23** wooden skewers **24** all-purpose glue **25** marker pen **26** pencil **27** ruler **28** paper clips **29** mini single hole punch and mat

Wire, ribbon, and tape

Most paper poms will need to be secured with some kind of wire or ribbon, so keep a good selection of narrow ribbon and pretty colored string in your craft box. Many of the projects in the book use garden or florist's wire, which is most often green but can be found in other colors, too. Garlands and bunting are hung on ribbon, colored string, or garden twine so look in haberdashery shops, craft stores, and garden centers. Florist's tape (also known as stem tape) is a paper tape that releases its own adhesive when stretched and is used in many of the projects in this book, where a realistic flower effect is desired. Decorative masking tape such as washi tape is available in a range of colors and patterns and is used in many of the projects in this book.

Adhesives

We use clear all-purpose glue for many of the projects in this book, but white PVA glue can also be used. A hot glue gun is a really useful investment—once you have used one, you will find you can't live without it! They are widely available from craft and home-improvement stores and are perfect when you need to secure something quickly and easily.

Tools

You need very little specialist equipment for making paper poms, but there are a few things that are useful to have in your craft toolbox.

Cutting tools

It is really important to have a good pair of sharp scissors for cutting crisp lines. Spring-loaded scissors are ideal for cutting through multiple layers; look for ones that have an easy-grip handle. At the studio we keep our scissors in tip-top condition by regularly spraying them with lubricant—simply coat the scissors in the open position, making sure you get the oil into the screw/nut. Leave for a few hours and then wipe off with a soft cloth. You will also be wiping away any tiny paper fibers—these minute traces of paper will eventually blunt your blades. Try not to get water on the scissors to prevent rusting and periodically tighten the screw. Keep a spare pair of old scissors that you use just use for cutting wire and card—only use your best scissors for your papers. Fancy-edge scissors are great for cutting decorative edges.

A rotary cutter is a tool generally used by quilters for cutting through layers of fabric. However, it can also be very useful when cutting multiple strips of paper. Use with a self-healing cutting mat—ideally with a grid so that you can cut straight lines to the correct dimensions. A craft knife with a retractable blade is useful for making short, sharp cuts—again, always use with a cutting mat.

Hole punches and fasteners

Thanks to the huge phenomenon of decorative scrapbooking, there is now have an excellent selection of products readily available on the market that are a great addition to any craft toolbox. Single hole punches are perfect for making perfect round holes through which to thread your ribbon or twine for garlands and bunting. Mini grommet (eyelet) makers will add a professional and neat finish to your projects. The grommets or eyelets come in a variety of sizes and are small, flanged brass tubes that reinforce punched-out holes and prevent unwanted rips or tears in your projects. Mini brads (paper fasteners) are just smaller versions of the fasteners you find in office supplies catalogs and come in lots of pretty colors and shapes.

Other useful equipment

Many of the things you will need to make the projects in this book are ordinary household items that you are likely to have already. These include food coloring (for dyeing coffee filters), modeling clay, and polystyrene cups (used for the Giant Daffodils on page 82), pencil, ruler, marker pen, wooden skewers, clothespins, paper clips, paintbrush and paints, and containers for paint, glue, or dye—recycled yogurt containers are ideal for this.

chapter one

poms and
hanging decorations

Make your very own stylish and classic paper poms for any party or celebration, using techniques that will impress your guests and make them think you've got a professional stylist or decorator working for you. Within the pages of this chapter, you will learn creative crafts and unexpected ways of turning different types of paper into beautiful decorations for the home or even a larger venue. Many of the projects can be combined to create an amazing backdrop, such as the Horizontal Fringe Twists on page 26 and the Rosette Fans on page 29. Add flourishes to the tops of cakes with the simple but effective Mini Pom Cake Toppers on page 23 or prettify your table with the Place Setting Daisies on page 20.

paper poms

Paper pom-poms started out as a form of Mexican papercraft—they were paper flowers, used to adorn shrines on the Day of the Dead and to decorate at "Cinco de Mayo" (Spanish for fifth of May) parties. In the 1970s, these vibrant paper flowers grew popular in the UK and US and evolved into paper poms. Fast-forward 35 years and, with the help of Martha Stewart, they are now a feature of the US bridal and party market, albeit with a modern and stylish approach. These are one of the most versatile paper decorations that you will find in this book. They can be used for any celebration and made in any color or size. Hang them from ceilings, beams, or curtain rails, or add them to a wall display, while smaller poms make great Christmas tree decorations. Once you have mastered your first paper pom, you'll want to make them for any celebration.

You will need

(makes 1 pom, 14in / 35cm in diameter)

8 sheets 20 x 30in (50 x 75cm) colored tissue paper

60in (1.5m) white or colored ribbon, ¼in (5mm) wide (alternatively you can use fishing line)

Scissors

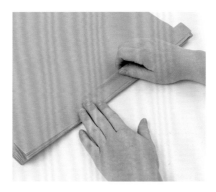

1 Lay out your eight sheets of tissue paper on top of each other and cut them in half—you should be able to use an existing fold line as a guide to cut them evenly in two. Place all the sheets together (you should now have 16 layers of paper). Starting at one of the shorter ends and keeping the stack of paper together, fold over approximately 1¼in (3.5cm).

2 Turn the stack of paper over and make the next fold, using the first fold you made as a guide. Continue in this way, making concertina-style folds along the whole length of paper. Make sure the folds are even—you will soon get to know how wide 1¼in (3.5cm) is by eye! Don't worry if you end on a "half" fold, as this can simply be trimmed off.

Keep the tissue-paper trimmings from rounding the ends and use them as confetti!

3 Tie your length of ribbon around the middle of the pleated tissue paper to hold the folds in place.

4 Now you need to cut the ends of each fold into rounded petals. Work on just one fold at a time to make cutting easier and to stop the paper from tearing or scrunching up. Start by cutting a diagonal line about ¼in (5mm) from one corner of the fold and make the cut about 1¼in (3.5cm) long. Use the first cut as your guide for the subsequent cuts.

5 When you have made all the diagonal cuts, start cutting the ends into rounded shapes. Pinch the top of the folds between your thumb and forefinger and use your forefinger top knuckle as a guide for the scissors to rest on.

6 Repeat steps 4 and 5 at the other end of your pleated tissue paper. Make sure your pom is even on both sides by checking the ribbon placement or by fanning open the pom and seeing if it looks unbalanced.

7 You are now ready to unfurl! Fan out both sides of the pom and pull up the first layer on either side outward and as far into the central knot as possible. If the first layer isn't pulled up into the center point, it will be difficult to open the pom into a lovely round shape and the result will be a slightly oval-shaped pom.

8 Keep pulling up the layers on this first "quarter" of the pom until they are all opened out.

9 Repeat steps 7 and 8 on the opposite side.

10 Turn the pom over and repeat steps 7–9 until all the layers are open and you have a lovely, even, round ball.

Try these other pom sizes—the following all use 20 x 30in (50 x 75cm) sheets of tissue paper

- For a 20in (50cm) pom: use 17 sheets. Do not fold and cut in half and fold into concertina folds as above.
- For a 10in (25cm) pom: use three sheets. Fold and cut in half, then fold and cut again so that you have a stack of 12 sheets that are 10 x 15 in (25 x 38cm). The concertina folds should be around ¾in (2cm) wide.
- For a 7in (18cm) pom: use two sheets. Fold and cut in half three times so that you end up with 16 layers of tissue paper. You will find that there are too many layers in this pom, so remove four layers, leaving 12 in the stack. The concertina folds should be around ½–¾in (1.5–2cm) wide.
- For a 4in (10cm) pom: use the four layers that were removed from the 7in (18cm) pom above and fold and cut in half to create eight layers. The concertina fold size should be around ¼–½in (8–10mm) wide.
- For a 2¾in (7cm) pom: use half a sheet, folded and cut into 16 layers that are approximately 3½ x 4in (8.5 x 10cm).

rosette snowflakes

This is a simple, quick, and effective decoration that can be hung in the windows or on your Christmas tree. Use plain white printer paper for classic white snowflakes or any colorful papers—even metallics—to brighten up your festive setting.

**You will need
(for 1 snowflake)**

1 sheet of 200gsm paper, cut to 6 x 10in (15 x 25cm)

Narrow ribbon or fishing line for hanging

Scissors

Clear all-purpose glue

Paper clip

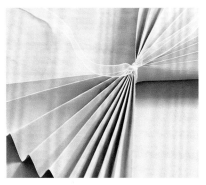

1 Place your paper in front of you with the short end facing you. Start making small concertina folds, about ½in (1cm) wide, along the short edge of the paper. Keep folding until you get to the end of the paper. Tie your ribbon or fishing line tightly around the center of the folds.

2 Using your scissors, cut semicircles, triangles, and half diamonds randomly along each fold. It's good to experiment with simple projects like this to see what can be achieved with different cuts.

3 Now cut each folded end into a pointed shape. Fan out the two sides to see if you have made enough cuts in your snowflake; you can always snip out more shapes if you feel it needs it. All your snowflakes should look different but as if they're from the same snowstorm!

4 Move the knot in the ribbon or fishing line so that it is placed in the middle of the last fold—this will allow your snowflake to hang vertically rather than horizontally. Then use clear all-purpose glue to stick the ribbon along the paper from the center to the end of the fold.

5 Stick the opposite fold down over the top of the ribbon to conceal it within the snowflake.

6 Fan out the two sides and secure together with a paper clip. Doing this means that you can pack the snowflakes away flat—not only will they be perfect when you take them out the following year, but they will also take up less storage space.

Try making your snowflakes out of colored cellophane sheets or vintage sewing-pattern paper for unusual effects.

place setting daisies

We made these daisies to decorate our Easter table—they will last for many years and can be taken out of your decorations box year after year. You can use any paper for the flower petals, but you'll need a softer, lighter tissue paper for the flower centers. You can make these in a variety of sizes; one sheet of US letter size (A4) paper will make nine 2½in (6cm) daisies or four 3½in (9cm) ones.

You will need

White paper for the petals (use printer paper, tissue paper, or even old letters!)

Yellow tissue paper for the centers

Scissors

10in (25cm) garden wire or string, or narrow ribbon (⅛in/3mm wide)

Wooden toothpick or tweezers (optional)

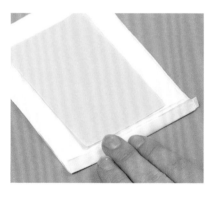

1 Cut the white paper into a rectangle 5 x 3½in (13 x 9cm). If you are using tissue paper, you will need five or six layers; if you are using printer paper, one layer will do. Now cut your daisy centers from the yellow tissue paper—you will need four layers each 3¾ x 2½in (9.5 x 6cm). Stack the white paper together with the yellow layers on top.

2 Starting at one of the shorter ends, make a small fold ¼in (5mm) wide. Holding all the papers together, carefully turn the stack of paper over and make a second fold back over the first fold.

3 Continue making these very small concertina folds until you can't fold any more. Use something heavy, such as a pair of scissors, to weight down the folds while you pick up your wire, string, or ribbon.

4 Wrap your wire, string, or ribbon around the mid-point of the pleated paper and tie in a secure knot. Leave the ends of the ribbon long so that they become part of the decoration—they can also be used for tying around napkins or votives.

5 Now cut small round shapes into the ends of the folds. First make a small snip about ½in (1cm) long into one of the folds at one end—this will make it easier to cut the rounded ends. Repeat at the other end.

6 Then cut small round shapes into the ends of the folded paper stack.

7 Fan out the folds of the daisy centers by teasing out the layers one by one toward the knot. If you find this too fiddly to do with your fingers, use a toothpick or a pair of tweezers. Fluff all of the layers—if they seem too long, use scissors to trim them.

8 To separate the petals, snip just over halfway down each fold crease toward the center of the daisy.

9 Ease the flower into shape, trimming the curves on the tips of the petals if necessary. Use to decorate your place settings or tie around rolled napkins.

You only need scraps of paper to make these daisies, so save any offcuts and leftovers from other projects to make them.

mini pom cake toppers

Cupcakes are as popular as ever and there are endless ways to decorate them. These little flirty, feathery globes are a unique idea and when popped into the middle of a cupcake or a trio of cakes will certainly make an impression. As with a lot of pretty things, they can be a little fiddly to make but you can use them more than once—just make sure you snip off the end of the pop stick each time for hygiene reasons.

1 Fold the sheet of tissue paper in half and then into quarters, the fold again along the shortest side three times until you have a folded strip of paper about 6 x 2½in (15 x 6cm).

2 Place the circle template on the folded tissue paper and draw around it. Repeat as many times as will fit. Carefully cut out the circles to create a stack of tissue circles.

3 If you are worried about scattering the tissue paper circles as you cut them, a useful tip is to make a small hole in the center of each circle before you cut them out and then push a brad (paper fastener) through each one. Open out the two pins at the back—the tissue circles are now securely fastened together.

You will need

(makes 4 cake toppers)

1 sheet 20 x 30in (50 x 75cm) tissue paper

Template on page 122

4 mini brads (paper fasteners)

Sharp scissors

4 wooden skewers or cake pop sticks, 6in (15cm) long

Double-sided foam tape, ½in (1cm) wide

Decorative or colored washi tape (optional)

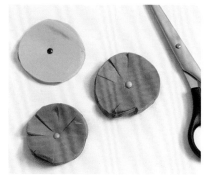

4 Using the template as a guide, make straight cuts in the circles with the tips of your scissors, cutting from the outside edge in toward the center. Cut as close as you can to the brad. You'll find that the paper skews as you cut the straight lines, but this is totally fine as it helps with the feathering effect.

5 Cut a ⅝in (1.5cm) length of double-sided foam tape, peel off the backing tape on one side, and wrap the sticky side around the top of a wooden skewer or cake pop stick. Peel off the second layer of tape backing. Then find the central point of your paper stack and push the taped end of the stick into the middle of the layers of paper as far as it will go. Pull down three or four layers of paper over the top of the stick and gently squeeze the layers over the tape until it feels secure.

Try this

To make a slightly larger pom cake topper, simply fold your tissue paper into a wider strip and use a larger circle as your template. You could also make smaller sizes—just use a smaller circle!

6 If you want to decorate your stick, cut a length of washi tape and start wrapping it around the stick, starting at the top. Alternatively you could just add one or two horizontal strips of tape to create bands of color, rather than cover the whole area.

7 Using your fingers or the end of one of your sticks, separate the layers of tissue paper to fluff up the "disc" into a ball shape. However, if you are posting these to a friend or traveling to a party with them, you may want to leave the fluffing until just before you insert the sticks into the cakes.

horizontal fringe twists

Vertical drops of Italian crepe paper with horizontal fringing hang beautifully when the crepe paper is twisted a few times—the fronds float and wave, just like sea kelp in the deep blue sea! This project would create a lovely modern backdrop for any party or celebration. Or you could simply hang them along an empty wall in your house—hallways, bedrooms, lounges, and garden rooms would all benefit from a bit of movement and glamor. You could also use this decoration as a room divider in bedrooms or lounges.

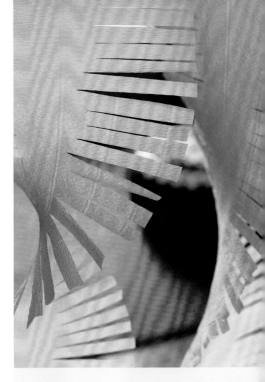

You will need

1 x 2¾yd (2.5m) roll of Italian crepe paper

Scissors

Pale or white ribbon for hanging, approximately ¼in (5mm) wide

Clear all-purpose glue

1 Cut the roll of tissue paper into two equal halves. The easiest way to do this is to unroll a little at a time and use one of the natural lines in the crepe paper as a guide.

2 Take each length of crepe paper and pull out the stretch (you may find this easier with two people!). This will take a little time, but it will double or even quadruple the length of your paper, depending on what type you use.

3 Fold the paper back into loose folds of two or three layers (or whatever your scissors can cope with) and start cutting straight lines about 4in (10cm) long toward the center of the paper. Space the cuts about ½ in (1cm) apart. Keep folding so that you are cutting through several layers at the same time, and continue until you reach the end of the paper. Now repeat all the way down the opposite side.

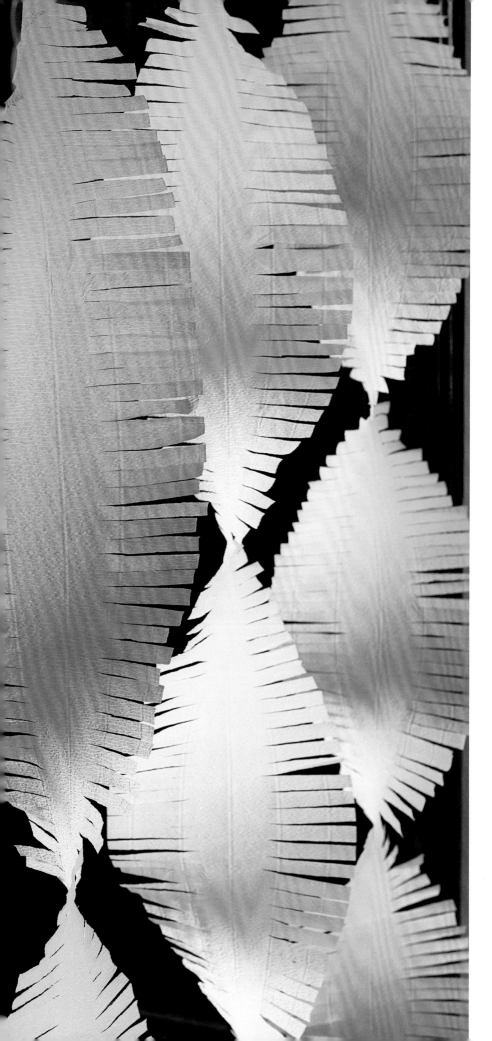

4 Cut the fringing into your desired lengths and then cut a length of ribbon approximately three times the width of the paper. Fold over about ½in (1cm) at one end of the crêpe paper and apply a line of glue inside the fold. Find the mid-point of your ribbon and place it inside the fold, then press down firmly to secure. Allow to dry before hanging.

5 To hang your lengths of paper fringes, attach to the ceiling, making sure they are at least 8in (20cm) away from the wall so that you can twist the garland. Hold the bottom of the drop and twist the garland a few times until you are happy with the effect.

rosette fans

This delightful and satisfying project will give you an instant party pop and is so easy to do that you could almost leave it to the very last minute before your guests arrive! Clusters of these fans can be displayed together, either suspended from ceilings or flat against a wall. We usually leave the tips uncut, but shapes can be cut into the ends to form petals if you wish. As you get used to the technique, you can try experimenting with newspaper, wallpaper, and even materials like fabric tulle and netting!

1 Lay two of the tissue sheets together, short end to short end. Overlap the edges by ¾in (2cm). Glue along the overlap and press down so that the paper is smooth. Make sure that the paper is fully glued down, with no gaps. Leave to dry while you repeat with the other two sheets. You should end up with two long sheets, approximately 59in (148cm) long.

Try making your rosette fans out of newspaper sheets glued end-to-end, instead of tissue paper. You could even paint the newspaper for a graphic, urban look.

2 Lay the first sheet over the second and stack neatly. Holding the two layers firmly—but not so tightly that you scrunch the paper—fold over to make a ¾in (2cm) wide crease. Then, instead of flipping over the sheets, we use the "double fold" concertina technique as follows: hold the first fold that you made (thumbs under the paper and fingers placed on top), raise the paper up toward you by around 2in (5cm) and push a parallel line and fold under with your thumbs until the midpoint of the paper meets the line of the first fold that you made. With each double fold that you make, press the creases down so that you form a nice, sharp, clean line. Try to keep all of the lines straight and even, as it can be easy to skew the folds.

You will need

(makes one 20in/50cm diameter rosette)

4 sheets 20 x 30in (50 x 75cm) tissue paper

Glue stick

Narrow ribbon or fishing line (for hanging)

Scissors

Clear all-purpose glue

Paper clips

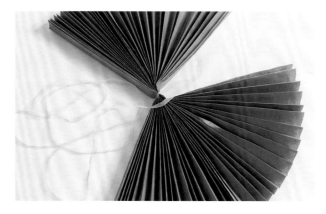

3 Repeat until all your folds are completed. (When you get to the glued parts of the paper, you should be able to continue folding without any problems.) Tie your ribbon or fishing line around the center point and secure in place with a double knot.

4 If you find that the tissue paper is uneven at the ends of the concertina folds, all you need to do is trim them flat with scissors. Alternatively, cut petal shapes into the ends if desired.

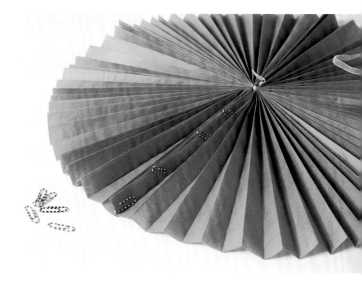

5 Move the knot in the ribbon so that it is placed in the middle of the last fold. This will ensure that the rosette will hang vertically rather than horizontally. Fan out the first two halves and make sure that the ends meet; if they do not, re-trim at this point. Using clear all-purpose glue, run a line of glue along one side of the last fold. Lay the ribbon on top of the glue—this way it will be sandwiched between the two layers. This will be the top of your rosette.

6 Pull both fan sides down until they meet and carefully press down together. Now fan out the opposite side and use paper clips to secure the folds of paper at the ends of the rosette.

scored stars

The inspiration for these stars is taken from some large metal stars that I spotted in a reclamation yard—rusted and weathered, but beautiful nevertheless. Ours are made from mirrored card but old greeting cards would work extremely well here. This star can be hung individually on a Christmas tree or make several and hang at different heights in a cluster at any time of year, party or no party.

You will need

Templates on page 118

Mirrored, plain, or patterned card or good-quality (180gsm) paper

Pencil

Scissors or craft knife

Metal ruler

Scoring tool, such as a bone folder—alternatively use the non-sharp side of your scissors

⅛in (3mm) punch tool or mini hole punch

Narrow ribbon, ⅛in (3mm) wide, for hanging

1 Position one of the Scored Star templates on your chosen card and draw around it with a pencil.

2 Repeat if desired and then cut your stars out, using either scissors or a craft knife.

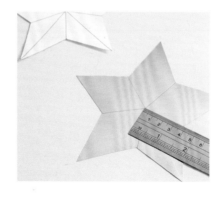

3 Turn the stars over and, following the template, use a metal ruler and pencil to drawn the straight lines from the points to the center on the back of the star. Make sure your lines meet exactly at the mid-point of the star (otherwise you'll lose the crispness of the form). Turn your star over and lightly draw in the shorter lines, from the inverted corners to the center.

4 Take your scissors or scoring tool and metal ruler and start to score along your longer pencil lines. Do this with a little pressure, but not so much that you will tear the paper or card. Turn over and repeat on the shorter lines.

5 Using a little force with your fingers, squeeze and fold either side of one of the longer scored lines so that they are pushed backward. Do this on all five points. Then turn over and repeat on the shorter lines.

6 To hang the star, punch a small hole at the top of one of the star's tips and thread through your ribbon. A mixture of large and small stars looks good when hung as a display.

honeycomb ball

These handmade honeycomb balls are made from recycled magazines or newspapers, so are the perfect eco deco. Make them for birthdays, Christmas, or any party you like! You can use standard-size magazine pages, larger newspaper sheets, or even a broadsheet newspaper for a giant ball!

You will need

2 old magazines (look for ones that have about 90 pages and are secured with staples)

Ruler

Marker pen

Clear all-purpose glue

Masking tape

Thick paper or thin cardstock

Scissors

Paper clips

Ribbon or string

1 Lay one of the magazines in front of you and open the first page. On the right-hand page, use your ruler and marker pen to draw a series of horizontal lines that are 2in (5cm) apart, starting near the top of the page. Apply a line of glue along each marked line. Turn the page and press it down firmly, then draw another series of lines on the next right-hand page, this time alternating the lines so that they are between the lines drawn on the previous page. Continue working like this through the magazine, alternating the lines each time. You may want to create a "grid" to help you: simply tape a piece of masking tape down the right-hand side and mark it at 1in (2.5cm) intervals, alternating between dots and stars. Repeat with the second magazine and leave both to dry for at least 2 hours.

2 Now that your magazine honeycombs are complete, it's time to make the honeycomb ball. Decide how big you want your ball to be and find a suitable round object, such as a plate. (You will need to make sure that the staples that hold the magazine pages together are within the circle.) Draw around this onto thick paper or thin cardstock to make a circle. Fold or cut your circle in half to create a perfect semicircle and then use this to draw a semicircle on each magazine, making sure the straight edge is lined up with the edge of the magazine. Cut out.

3 Glue one of the semicircles on top of the other and leave to dry. Open out both semicircles to reveal the honeycomb pages and gently bring the two outer edges together and secure with paper clips.

4 Glue a loop of ribbon or string into the fold—this will be your hanging loop.

hanging pom heart

We are often asked by florists, chocolatiers, and top cake bakeries to make pom hearts to dress their shops and window displays. There is no reason why you shouldn't make these to display in the home—whether for a baby shower, christening, engagement party, or just to hang in a bedroom. The poms are quick to make, as there are no petals to cut, and we've made a relatively small heart shape from corrugated card. You can also buy 3-D heart shapes ready to decorate from craft stores, or you could even attach poms to a willow or hazel heart found in garden centers and home stores.

You will need

Template on page 119

Corrugated card

Cutting mat and craft knife

Narrow ribbon, for hanging

96in (240cm) florist's wire

Wire cutters

4 sheets 20 x 30in (50 x 75cm) tissue paper (1 sheet of paper will make 4 poms)

Scissors

Clear all-purpose glue or hot glue gun

1 Use the template on page 119 to draw a heart shape on your corrugated card. Cut out the heart shape, using a cutting mat and craft knife, and then cut out the middle section, so that you have a slim frame.

2 Make a small hole at the top of the heart and thread your hanging ribbon through the hole. Tie to secure.

If both sides of the heart are likely to be seen, make double the amount of poms so that you can attach them to the back of the heart, too.

3 Cut the florist's wire into 16 equal 6in (15cm) pieces with wire cutters and set to one side. Working with a couple of sheets of tissue paper at a time, fold, crease, and cut the tissue into smaller rectangles that are 3½ x 5in (9 x 12.5cm), keeping your edges straight and neat. Count out eight small sheets into 16 separate neat piles of paper. Take one stack of tissue paper sheets and fold over ½in (1cm) along the shortest length. Continue making concertina folds until you get to the end of the tissue paper, then wrap a piece of florist's wire around the center of the fold. Twist to secure. Repeat to make 16 poms in total.

4 Fluff the poms. Hold the pom at the place where the wire is twisted (this will be the back of your pom). Tease out the first layer that is facing you. Pull this as far as you can toward the center of the pom. Repeat on the other side. Then tease and fluff up the remaining layers, all of them away from the back of the pom. Trim any long pieces of wire with wire cutters.

5 Take one pom and glue it to the "dip" in the heart shape, using clear all-purpose glue or a hot glue gun. Continue adding poms, bearing in mind that you will need an equal amount on each side of the heart.

6 Fluff up any layers that may have been flattened. Your heart is now ready to display.

3-D star mobile

This is a very sweet mobile project that you can vary by adding other shapes and elements to the display—think trees, apples, pears, or hearts. Embellish it further by drawing and cutting out small fairies to hang alongside or stick onto the shapes that are on the mobile.

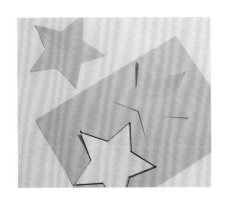

1 Use the template on page 118 to draw and cut out 64 stars from your colored paper (you will need eight stars for each shape).

2 Fold each shape in half and press it firmly to make a sharp crease. Stack the shapes on top of each other so that all the edges line up. Holding your stack of stars firmly together, take your stapler and staple along the creased line in the center of the star. You should now have something that resembles a small star-shaped book.

You will need

Template on page 118

Several sheets of colored printer paper (180gsm or less)

Scissors

Stapler

Thin twine

2 green garden support canes, each 18in (45cm) long

Washi tape

Thumb tack (drawing pin)

You could add painted table tennis balls, beads, or small bells to your mobile for extra detail—just make sure the weights all balance.

3 To create a hanging loop: staple the top of one of the star points, positioning the stapler so that only half of the staple goes through the paper. Cut a length of thin twine and pass the end through the staple loop; knot to secure.

4 Gently tease out and arrange the layers of the star so that they fan out equally to create a 3-D shape.

5 Wrap the garden canes with colored washi tape, so that the whole of each cane is covered.

6 Using your thumb tack (drawing pin), push a hole into each covered garden cane, about 1in (2.5cm) from one end. Then make another hole, 1in (2.5cm) from the first hole and repeat at the other end of the cane so that you have four holes in each cane. Now add one central hole for hanging that is slightly larger than the others. (Make sure this hole is in the very center of the rod, so that the mobile is balanced when hung.)  Attach your mobile shapes to each rod so that they hang at different lengths: thread the twine through the holes and then tie a double knot when you are happy with the distance from the shape to the hanging rod. Attach the second cane to the first with twine, at a height that you are happy with.

top hat piñata

Piñatas are all the rage at parties now, whether for adults or children. Piñatas can be any shape you like, so why not a top hat? Even better, once you have popped it to reveal the goodies inside, it can be worn as a party hat! This project is so easy that you could make one for each of your guests, so that everyone gets to eat the treats inside and wear a hat, too. We have used gold foil for a traditional look, but you could decorate your hat to go with a specific party theme or add paper to make stripes or polka dots. This piñata has a pull string, so there's no need to smash your handiwork with a stick—and you can obviously use it again.

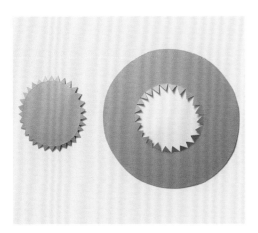

1 Use the templates on page 122 to cut the brim and lid for your hat out of cardstock. If you are using pre-glittered paper, then stick this to your card with spray adhesive before you cut around the template. Make small triangular cuts into the inside edge of the brim and around the lid.

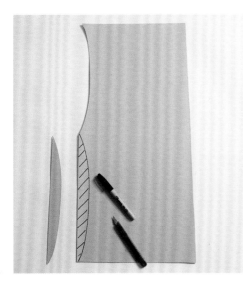

2 Cut a 24½ x 11in (62 x 28cm) rectangle for the body of the hat. Cut two narrow curves along one long side, as shown. This will create the wave in the brim of the hat when attached.

✳ ✳ ✳

You will need

Templates on pages 122–123

2 large sheets of cardstock, roughly 24 x 36in (60 x 90cm)

Spray adhesive (optional)

Scissors

Stapler

Duct tape

Hot glue gun

Thin cardstock for the hat base (cereal box card is ideal)

Cutting mat and craft knife

4in (10cm) narrow ribbon for the trapdoor, plus extra for hanging (optional)

2 sheets gold foil, 24 x 33in (60 x 83cm)

3 Form the main body of the hat into a cylinder, overlapping the edges by ½in (1cm) and making sure that it will still fit neatly over the brim of the hat. Staple the cylinder at each end (as far in as your stapler will reach) to hold in place.

4 Use duct tape to tape over the join, making sure you overlap by at least 2½in (6cm) at either end—fold this overlapping tape over to the inside of the cylinder.

5 Position the lid of the hat on top of the non-curved end of the cylinder and start to bend down the triangles that you cut earlier so that they cover the outside edge of the cylinder. Hot glue gun these in place.

6 Place the hat upright and repeat to secure the body of the hat to the brim. Tape over all the joins with duct tape.

7 Now make the base of the hat and the trapdoor pull. Use the template on page 122 to cut the base from slightly thinner cardstock. Use a craft knife and cutting mat to cut around three sides of the trapdoor and gently score the fourth side. Pierce a hole in the center of the trapdoor and thread your ribbon through the hole so that you have a loop about 1in (2.5cm) long. Hot glue gun the ribbon in place.

8 Position the base over the bottom of the hat and hot glue gun it in place.

9 Cut several strips (at least 10) of gold foil that are 28 x 1½in (70 x 4cm) and then make small vertical snips about ½in (1cm) apart to make the piñata fringing.

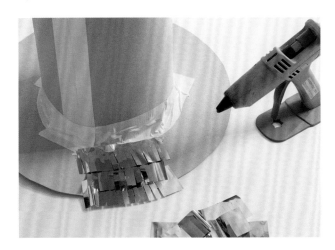

10 Using the hot glue gun, start to glue the fringe around the brim of the hat until it is completely covered. Cover the top of the hat with straight lines of fringing, wrapping the edge of the fringe over the edge of the top of the hat. Then start at the base of the hat and work your way up the hat until it is completely covered.

11 Turn the hat on its end and cover the underside with gold fringing, making sure you can still open the trapdoor. Fill your piñata with sweets or confetti, tease the trapdoor into its hole, and your piñata top hat is complete! If you want to hang your piñata, attach a length of ribbon to the top of the hat using a hot glue gun.

chapter two

garlands and *bunting*

The makes in this chapter will transform any room and give your party a great atmosphere, as well as that all-important wow factor. Garlands, when made in long lengths and draped across a room, can transform spaces instantly and at minimal or no cost. Create a whimsical and dreamy setting for a wedding with the Tassel Garland on page 53 or the Rose Garland on page 70. Kids of all ages will love the Circus Puppets on page 63, while the Vintage Book Bunting on page 66 or the Shooting Stars on page 74 will look fantastic in any child's bedroom. Get your scissors ready and let your imagination run wild!

leaves on twine

This is a delicate and delightful garland which could be left up all year round! Here the rosebush-type leaves have been teamed with some beautiful giant roses (see page 87). You could also use it to dress an outdoor summer party: note that if the paper gets wet, the color may run from the leaves, but this could add a different element to the design! For the leaves I used doublette crepe paper that has a different color on each side, but any make or type is fine—you could even sponge plain white paper with green paint. The roses are made from waterproof Italian crepe paper.

✳ ✳ ✳

You will need

Template on page 122

Pencil

Crepe paper

Scissors

Fancy-edge scissors or pinking shears (optional)

Seagrass twine or garden string

Hot glue gun

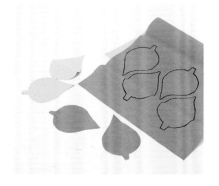

1 Use the template to draw several leaf shapes on the crepe paper. Make sure you position them on the horizontal grain of the paper, as you need to be able to stretch them later. Don't worry if you position the leaves over a fold in the paper, as any folds will disappear when the leaves are stretched. You will need eight leaves per yard (meter) of garland. Cut them out using regular craft scissors.

2 Use the fancy-edge scissors or pinking shears to trim the leaves or tear with your fingers to get a really rustic look. Tearing will also pull the stretch from the crepe, producing very unique leaves!

3 Stretch and shape the leaves as desired by pulling along the grain of the paper.

4 Use a hot glue gun to fix the leaves to the twine or string, spacing them about 4in (10cm) apart. Hand, drape, or wear—whatever takes your fancy! To add a giant rose, see pages 87–89.

cupcake flowers

We all have spare cupcake cases in the store cupboard, whether white, plain, or patterned. Add a spare set of fairy lights and a handful of loom bands and you can create a cheery garland to be hung in the porch, hallway, kitchen, or around fireplaces. If your cupcake cases are white, simply paint or dye them with tea or food coloring to make a unique, "one of a kind" festoon. Patterned cases are great to use, as the print will show through on both sides when the lights are on. Try mixing plain and patterned cases together.

1 To make the main flower: take one of your larger cases and fold it in half. Fold it in half again twice until you have a cone shape, and then cut round petal shapes from one end. When the case is opened out, you should have an eight-petal flower.

2 A 16-petal flower is made in the same way, except the case is folded into sixteenths. You can also create different effects by cutting pointed petals instead of rounded ones.

3 To make the outer leaves of the flower, take a large case—preferably green in color—and fold it twice before cutting pointed shapes into it. This will give you four pointed leaves. Keep going until you have enough flower cases to fit to your fairy lights.

4 Carefully cut a cross in the center of each paper case using your craft knife and cutting mat. This will allow the cases to slip over the fairy lights.

❉ ❉ ❉

You will need

Paper cupcake cases in assorted colors and sizes (2–3 liners for each bulb)

Scissors

Craft knife and cutting mat

String of fairy lights

Loom bands

Rip or tear the petals, rather than cutting, to give these little light shades a boho look.

5 Tie a loom band around the base of each fairy light. Then gently push your newly cut cupcake cases over the bulb until they rest against the loom band.

6 Arrange the cupcake cases as you want them and then secure with another loom band tied in front of the cases to stop them from coming undone.

tassel garland

Simple tissue twists transform flat sheets of tissue paper into full, elegant tassels. This whimsical decoration trend started in the United States as an alternative to tissue-paper poms and is a firm favorite with us. The colors that you choose make all the difference to the overall effect—hot pinks, blues, and yellows give a real carnival vibe, whereas muted pastel tones make an elegant garland with a "vintage" feel. The great thing about these garlands is that you can make them as long or as short as you need. Try criss-crossing the garlands across a room or outdoor marquee, or hang against a flat wall to create a pretty installation—or simply tie around the back of your dining chairs for a subtle dinner-party decoration.

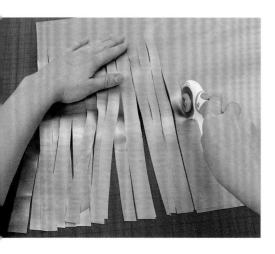

1 Take a sheet of tissue paper and fold it in half (short end to short end). Place on your cutting mat and use the rotary cutter to cut vertical strips 2½ in (6cm) from the fold line and ½in (1cm) apart. If your cutting mat has guidelines, you may find it easier and safer to follow these.

Why not use sheets of tissue paper that you may have stashed away from clothes or gift packaging? For best results when using folded sheets, iron them flat before you start, using a low heat setting and no steam.

You will need

(makes 1 garland, 2¾yd/2.5m long)

10 sheets 20 x 30in (50 x 75cm) gold tissue paper

Cutting mat

Rotary cutter

Wooden skewer or cake pop stick, approximately 8in (20cm long)

2¾yd (2.5 m) ribbon or lace, ¾in (2cm) wide

Masking tape

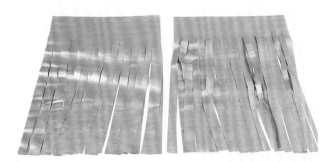

2 Continue along the sheet until you reach the end of the paper and then cut the paper vertically into two equal sections.

3 Repeat steps 1 and 2 with the remaining nine sheets of tissue paper. Once you have got used to the technique, try laying several sheets of paper together before you cut to help speed things up. You should now have 20 pieces of fringing.

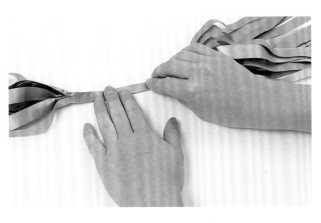

4 Take one of the pieces and open it out with the uncut center section in front of you. Tightly fold the center section into ¼in (5mm) folds. Repeat with all the pieces of fringing.

5 To create a loop in the tassel, fold the center section of the tassel over the skewer or stick and twist the paper firmly until the center section is twisted and you have a loop at the top. Repeat for all the tassels.

6 Finally, thread the tassels onto your ribbon or lace. The easiest way to do this is to attach the end of your ribbon to one end of your skewer or stick with some masking tape—like a giant needle and thread. Feed the stick and ribbon through the loop on each tassel until they are all on the ribbon.

7 To arrange your tassels, simply push them along the ribbon so that there is a gap of approximately 4in (10cm) between each one.

multi-leaf garland

These leafy garlands would make a beautiful backdrop for a fairies and elves party! You could even create a little woodland setting with toadstool cupcakes, chocolate mud cakes, and other delicious treats. Use multiple layers of different soft shades of green tissue paper for the best results. The lightweight tissue paper will move and sway in response to the slightest breeze—magical!

You will need

Templates on page 123

Several sheets of tissue paper—we used 4 shades of green

Pencil

Craft scissors

Hot glue gun or clear all-purpose glue

Seagrass twine, garden string, or narrow ribbon

Use small screw-in hooks or adhesive hooks to hang these to walls and ceilings without damaging the surface.

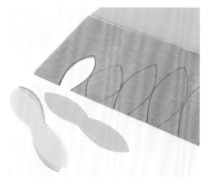

1 Use the templates on page 123 to cut out a selection of leaf shapes: you will need about 20 leaves per yard (meter) of garland. Lay three layers of tissue paper together and then fold over 10in (25cm). Position the templates with the flat edge on the fold, draw around them in pencil, and cut out.

2 Open out a leaf shape and apply a line of glue in the center, using either a hot glue gun or clear all-purpose glue.

3 Fold the leaf shape over the twine, string, or ribbon. Keep adding leaves, making them overlap each other so that the garland is packed with leaves.

snip shape streamers

These simple but beautiful garlands can be combined with the ornaments, tinsel, and fairy lights that you bring out every year. And what better paper to use than last year's Christmas gift wrap that you saved from the presents that you received? These are so easy to make that even children can join in! It's amazing how far the smallest scrap of paper will go in this very straightforward decoration. You can even glue small pieces of paper together end to end to create a lovely patchwork effect when you open the garland.

You will need
Selection of colorful giftwrap papers

Scissors

Glue stick

1 Iron out any wrinkles in your paper with your iron set to "no steam" and on the lowest heat. Cut the sheet into lengths approximately 4–5in (10–12cm) wide—don't make them too long or you may end up in a tangled mess. Take a strip and fold it in half lengthwise.

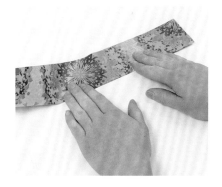

2 Using your scissors, make straight snips along one side of the folded paper. Each snip should be about 1½ in (4cm) long and ⅝in (1.5cm) apart. Repeat all the way along the length of the paper.

3 Now turn the paper around and snip along the opposite side. Again the snips should be 1½ in (4cm) long and should go in between the snips made on the opposite side. Repeat along the length of paper.

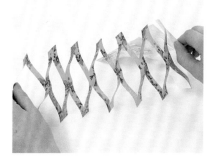

4 When you reach the end, carefully open out the folded paper. Gently stretch the paper, revealing the beautiful geometric cuts in your paper garland. Repeat the folding and cutting process on your other lengths, then glue them together to make longer streamers.

papel picado

I first saw papel picados in New Mexico 2009, on a road trip with my cousin. In a gift shop in Santa Fe we came across a huge area dedicated to El Dia de los Muertos (The Day of the Dead). I'd seen the iconic floral adorned and painted skeletons and skulls many times, but I'd never seen a picado before! I had just started making my poms and, knowing how delicate tissue paper is, was in awe of the intricate designs that were cut into each of the pennants, each one different to the next.

✻ ✻ ✻

You will need

Templates on page 125

Tracing paper

Pencil

Thin cardstock

Scissors

Several sheets of tissue paper in assorted colors

Mini clothespins or paper clips

Iron

Clear all-purpose glue or super-tacky PVA glue

Narrow ribbon

1 Trace one of the templates on page 125 onto a folded piece of thin cardstock. Cut it out and then use small sharp scissors to cut out the holes, folding the card as necessary to cut out the small shapes (see the step 5 photo on page 62).

2 Cut your tissue paper into smaller rectangles, approximately 10 x 5in (25 x 12.5cm). To save time cut several sheets together, but don't layer more than five or six sheets at a time.

3 Take a stack of five sheets and fold it in half. Fold your template in half and tuck the folded tissue inside the template. Use a couple of mini clothespins or paper clips to hold the template and tissue-paper layers together.

4 Start by cutting the scalloped edging—this will get you used to cutting through the layers and how to curve the scissors to achieve the slightly more complex inner shapes.

5 When you have completed the outer cuts, pick an inner shape and fold all of the layers again in such a way that you can get your scissors in to cut the shape out. Repeat this step until all the shapes have been cut away.

6 Open out your sheets and iron out any creases on a low heat with no steam setting. Try not to sweep the iron over the picado but press down instead, otherwise the paper tends to curl up at the edges.

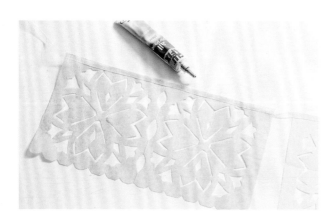 

7 Cut as many papel picados as you think you need—normally the picados are set quite close together, but you can space them out to suit your look. Lay out them out in your chosen order. Run a very thin line of glue along the top of one picado, then place your length of narrow ribbon (leaving some ribbon free on one side for hanging) on top. Press down gently so that the paper doesn't tear. Hang up the picado to stop it from sticking to the table while the glue is drying.

circus puppets

We chose a circus theme for this garland, because the silhouettes are so recognizable—think elephants, performing seals, trapeze artists, and lions. To make the figures even more fun, we added hats, balls, umbrellas, and other accessories. Good-quality patterned card (300gsm) or saved greeting cards are perfect for this, as you'll have lots of different designs to cut from, which can make some very interesting parts of the "puppets." We used mini brads (paper fasteners) to join heads, bodies, legs, and arms to one another—these come in lots of different colors and shapes and can be found in all good craft stores. They create a look of jointed puppets and also mean that you can reposition the different elements to suit each character.

1 Use the templates on pages 120–121 to cut out the pieces of your puppets, using a selection of different cards. Don't forget to include any accessories, such as umbrellas, hats, and balls. For the trapeze artist, you will need to cut a wooden skewer to the right length and then cover it in washi tape.

You will need

Templates on page 120–121

300gsm cardstock or greeting cards
(at least 15 sheets)

Scissors

Wooden skewers

Washi tape

Mini brads (paper fasteners)

Mini grommet (eyelet) tool and
grommets (eyelets)—optional

Baker's twine or colored string,
for hanging

2 Using the sharp tips of your scissors or brad (paper fastener), make small holes in your pieces, using the dots marked on the templates as a guide. These are positioned in such a way as to make the puppets hang properly. Push the brad through the hole and secure by bending back the two small tails until your pieces are joined together.

3 Decide how you would like your figure to hang and then pierce one or two small holes along the top of your puppet. We used a mini grommet (eyelet) tool, but you could use the sharp point of your scissors or the ends of a brad (paper fastener).

You could hang shapes on the high rope in between each character to add a bit more variety and busyness to the overall look of the scene—try circus balls, stars, and mustaches.

4 Pass your baker's twine or string through the holes. Repeat with the other figures you have created until you have a group of figures, ready to hang.

vintage book bunting

Have you ever found a lovely, old, but slightly tattered vintage book at a yard (boot) sale or thrift store that you just don't know what to do with? Don't let it sit on the shelf collecting dust—why not give it a new lease on life as a paper bunting decoration? Hang it for children's parties or use as a permanent decoration in their bedrooms. Any book will do—plain text will work, but if you can find books with some lovely old illustrations, even better!

You will need

(makes 8ft/2.5m of garland)

16 book pages

Craft knife (optional)

Card

Pencil

Scissors or pinking shears

Hole punch

Sticky tape

8ft (2.5m) narrow ribbon

If you can't bear to cut pages from a book, think about color photocopying them onto tea-stained paper for a superb vintage look.

1 Carefully remove the pages from the book, using a craft knife if necessary. Create a card template by cutting it to the size of one page, then cutting a triangle at one end. Use this template to cut all the pages the same shape.

2 When you have cut all the pages into pennants, take your hole punch and make a hole at each top corner of the pennant.

3 Decide what order you would like the pages to run. Wrap a small piece of sticky tape around one end of your ribbon—this will make it easier to thread through the holes (like a shoelace). Start threading the pages onto the ribbon, carefully moving the pennant to the other end of the tape.

4 Repeat until all your pennants have been threaded on, and then hang!

fringe bunting

This tissue paper fringe is a neater and much "denser" version of the tassel garland (see page 53)—it is much flatter, as there are no twists to the lengths. The great thing about this fringing is that once the vertical cuts have been made, it is super easy to cut contours, scallops, or curves into the fringe itself. As well as hanging overhead, it works well around the edges of tables, or several garlands can be layered together to create a stunning backdrop. Use it to dress a variety of parties and occasions and choose colors to suit your celebration, whether it's a summer party or a winter wedding.

You will need

(makes 3¼yd/3m of garland)

4 sheets 20 x 30in (50 x 75cm) tissue paper

Cutting mat

Scissors

Rotary cutter

Clear all-purpose glue

4¼yd (4m) narrow ribbon, ¼–½in (5–10mm) wide

1 Take a sheet of tissue paper and fold it in half, long side to long side. Your sheet should now measure 30 x 10in (75 x 25cm). Crease the fold so that it's crisp and sharp.

2 Place your paper on the cutting mat. Measure and mark a line ½in (1cm) from the folded edge with the rounded end of a pen top (something that won't tear the paper or leave a pen or pencil mark). Make a series of vertical cuts, ½in (1cm) apart, from the line you marked at the folded edge downward along the length of the paper. Repeat this on all four sheets of paper. (If you are feeling confident about cutting multiple sheets of paper in one stack or have used a rotary cutter before, then you could lay all of your sheets of paper down and cut all layers at the same time.)

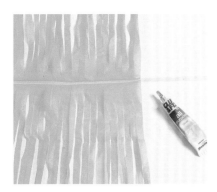

3 Take one of your cut sheets and carefully open the fringe to expose the inner crease. Do this on all four sheets. Place one sheet next to another and overlap the edges by about ½ in (1cm). Glue the overlapping tissue and repeat for the remaining two sheets. Only one side of the paper needs to be attached to the other.

4 Lay all the opened-out sheets out on your worktable or floor. Carefully run a line of glue along the crease mark of each sheet and then place your ribbon along the glue line. Repeat until all sheets have ribbon attached.

5 If you wish to cut shapes into the fringe, mark your lines or shapes with pencil and then use your scissors or rotary cutter to slice through it.

rose garland

There is something rather special about the spiraling pattern of a rose. This beautiful garland has roses made from coffee-filter petals, creating a whimsical and romantic rose with a retro feel. This garland is perfect for a wedding—it can be tied around the bride and groom's chairs at the reception, or draped around tables or staircases. Smaller versions would also make perfect bridesmaids' headdresses.

You will need

26 white or unbleached coffee filters, 8in (20cm) in diameter

Rubber gloves

Selection of food colorings (red, orange, yellow, and green)

Bowls or plastic pots for the dyes

Scissors

Templates on page 119

Wooden skewer

Hot glue gun

Secateurs

3¼yd (3m) seagrass twine

4¼yd (4m) florist's wire

1 Start by dividing up your coffee filters. Set aside two coffee filters to be dyed green for the leaves and then divide the rest equally between your chosen colors. Wear rubber gloves to protect your hands and then mix up your food coloring dyes (see page 115), making some more diluted colors too. Dip your filters into the dyes—pinks, oranges, and yellows for the roses, and green for the leaves. Wring them out and allow to dry. Experiment by adding splatters of the same color in a darker shade to some of your filters.

2 When the coffee filters are dry, use the template on page 119 to cut 12 petal shapes for each flower. You can fold a few filters together to cut several petals at once. Fold the green-dyed coffee filters in half and use the leaf template to cut three leaves for each flower, plus a few extra to add along the twine between each flower.

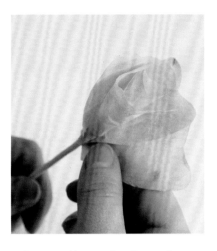

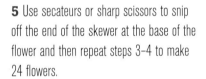

3 Make up the flowers, starting with the center of the rose. Add a dab of glue to the end of a wooden skewer with the hot glue gun, and roll one of the petals around, twisting it to cover the end of the skewer.

4 Continue adding petals, rolling each one around the skewer and gluing it in place. Fluff the petals outward to make the flowers wider.

5 Use secateurs or sharp scissors to snip off the end of the skewer at the base of the flower and then repeat steps 3–4 to make 24 flowers.

6 Wrap the end of your florist's wire several times around one end of the twine and secure it in place with a drop of glue from the hot glue gun. Start twisting the wire tightly around the twine at an angle until you get to the end of your twine. Wind the wire tightly around the end of the line and hot glue gun it in place.

7 To assemble the garland, mark sections along the line every 5in (12.5cm) with a small piece of tape. Take one of your flowers and hot glue it to the twine and wire rope line that you have made. Repeat this every 5in (12.5cm) along the twine. Glue three leaves around the base of each flower to hide the glue and then add more leaves to the twine between each flower.

To make a headdress

You will need eight or nine flowers, 1yd (1m) of florist's wire, and 24in (60cm) of seagrass twine. Follow step 6 above to make a wire and twine line that will fit around your head. Overlap the ends by 4in (10cm) and secure with florist's wire. Cover the ends of the wire with leaves. Attach flowers and leaves as in step 7.

shooting stars

This garland started out life as a single string of stars, which was very pretty, but it was missing something. So I added another two strings to create this effect of a shooting star flying across a room. It's a lovely garland to bring out at Christmas, birthdays, baby showers, or christenings. My little boy Jasper also loves to see these spangled, glittered, textured stars hanging above his cot.

You will need

Templates on page 118

6 sheets of 240gsm US letter size (A4) card, including silver, gold, and black glitter card

Scissors

Hand-held star punch (optional)

9¾yd (9m) baker's twine or colored string

Clear all-purpose glue

4in (10cm) narrow ribbon

4 thumb tacks (drawing pins)

1 Start by using the templates on page 118 to cut two large stars from silver card. Then cut 24 small stars from each of your silver, gold, and black cards, either using a star punch or by hand using the smaller star template. Cut your baker's twine or string into three equal lengths and glue the ends to the center of the back of one of the large stars, using clear all-purpose glue. Leave a 3in (8cm) gap before adding the first smaller star to the first strand, using clear all-purpose glue, then continue to add smaller stars at intervals of 2in (5cm).

2 Continue adding stars to complete the first strand, changing the color of the stars every eight stars. Repeat with the other two strands, to make three identical strands.

3 Fold your narrow ribbon in half to make a loop and glue it to the tip of the large star. Take the second large star and position it over the back of the first star. This will secure your hanging loop as well as hide the ends of the star tails.

4 The star and tails are ready to hang on the wall. Push a thumb tack (drawing pin) into the wall and hook the loop on your large star over it. Arrange the first tail so that it drapes nicely and fasten the end to the wall with another thumb tack (drawing pin). Repeat with the remaining two strands. Make a wish!

dreidel bunting

The shape of the boxes on this pretty bunting is based on the dreidel, a four-sided spinning top played with by children during the Jewish holiday of Hanukkah. Each side of the dreidel has a letter from the Hebrew alphabet, which, when put together, form an acronym (NGHS) for the Jewish saying, "a great miracle happened there." You'll need a cutting mat and craft knife here, as accurate cutting is necessary to create the perfect dreidel shape.

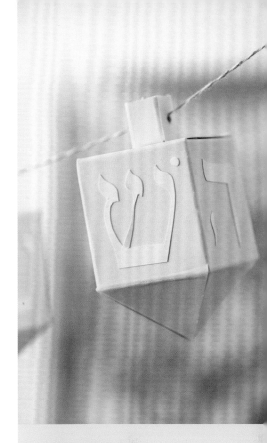

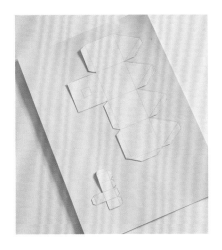

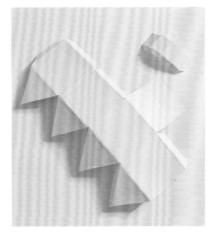

1 Photocopy the templates on page 124 and use them to draw the net for the box on the back of your thick paper. Use a sharp, retractable pencil and a metal ruler to create clean lines and then, working on a cutting mat, use a craft knife and metal ruler to cut out the net with perfectly straight lines. Repeat to make eight box nets.

2 The fold lines will need to be scored so that the boxes look crisp and sharp when made up. Do this with a scoring tool; alternatively you can use a sharp pencil instead, applying firm pressure when going over the lines. Use a metal ruler for accuracy. The dotted lines on the template are a guide and don't need to be traced onto your card. Gently fold along the scored lines.

You could cover the bases of the boxes with a metallic gold foil or paper so that the light catches them when they are spinning.

❋ ❋ ❋

You will need

Templates on page 124

Fine retractable pencil

Metal ruler

Several sheets of thick pale blue paper (320gsm)

Cutting mat

Craft knife

Scoring tool, such as a bone folder (optional)

Contrasting card or paper for the symbols

Scissors

Glue stick

Single hole punch

Baker's twine

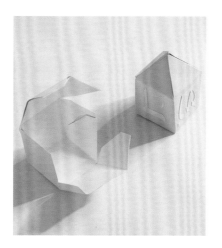

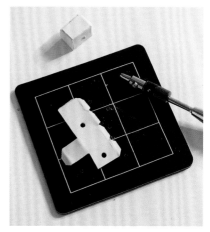

3 Trace the templates for the four symbols and cut them out in contrasting card or paper. Glue them centrally onto each face of the dreidel, following the order shown in the photograph.

4 Use your glue stick to spread glue onto the tabs of the main body and fold them in, one by one. Press gently to secure—you may need to hold closed for a few seconds.

5 Take the top section and use a hole punch to make two holes on the first and third tabs (this is so that you can thread the twine through). Make sure you position them in the center of the tabs. Glue the top section together as in the previous step.

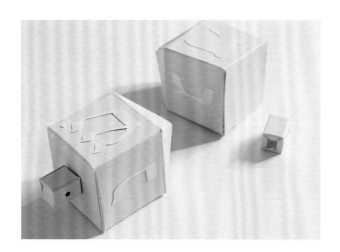

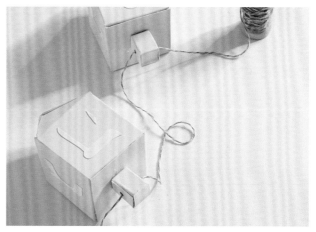

6 Glue the top section to the main body and hold it for a few seconds to secure.

7 Hang the dreidel on the twine by passing the line through the holes in the top section and position them in place along the line. Alternatively, thread the twine through each hole twice; this will stop them from sliding along the twine once you have hung them all on the line.

The dreidel game

The dreidel can easily be removed from the bunting to play the game. Here a few simple rules:

- At the beginning of each round, each player puts one game piece (often a sweet or chocolate coin) into the center. In addition, every time the pot is empty or has only one game piece left, every player should put one in the pot.
- When it's your turn, spin the dreidel once. Depending on the outcome, you give or get game pieces from the pot:

  Nun (נ) stands for "nisht" in Yiddish, which means "nothing." The player does nothing.

  Gimel (ג) stands for "gantz" in Yiddish, which means "everything." The player gets everything.

  Hay (ה) stands for "halb" in Yiddish, which means "half." The player gets half the pot. If there are an odd number of pieces in the pot, the player takes half, plus one.

  Shin (ש) stands for "shtel ayn" in Yiddish, which means "put in." The player adds a game piece to the pot.
- If you have no game pieces left, you are either out or may ask a player for a loan.
- When a player has won everything, the game is over!

✻✻✻✻✻✻✻✻✻✻✻✻✻✻✻✻✻✻✻✻✻✻✻✻✻✻✻✻✻✻

chapter three

centerpieces
and showstoppers

The projects in this chapter are designed to impress, whether you are adding some color and glamour to a room or decorating a venue or your home for a party. Be bold and make big creative statements, such as making the Giant Daffodils on page 82 for a garden party. Making an impact doesn't have to mean spending a lot of time and money on decorations—there are plenty of ideas here that are simple but effective, such as the Mini Mirror Cake Bunting on page 93 or the Tissue Bauble Heart on page 100. Dress your walls at home with Blossoms on a Branch, page 109, or cascades of Paper Wisteria, page 112.

✻✻✻✻✻✻✻✻✻✻✻✻✻✻✻✻✻✻✻✻✻✻✻✻✻✻✻✻✻✻

You will need

For the flower head

4 sheets 20 x 30in (50 x 75cm) pale yellow tissue paper (main flower)

3 sheets 20 x 30in (50 x 75cm) orange tissue paper (trumpet)

16in (40cm) florist's wire

Scissors

Clear all-purpose glue

For the base

Air-drying modeling clay

Large paper coffee cup

4ft (1.2m) bamboo pole

44 x 20in (110 x 50cm) corrugated cardboard

Duct tape

Green tissue paper

Soft paintbrush

PVA glue

Small screwdriver

For the leaves

Plastic wrap (cling film)

Masking tape

Small bowl

2 sheets 20 x 30in (50 x 75cm) green tissue paper

Green florist's wire

Template on page 125

giant daffodils

This project shows you how to make beautiful giant daffodils. We've given instructions for the stem and base, but the flower head works just as beautifully without it, attached to the backs of chairs, placed on a table as a centerpiece, or fixed around arbors and trellises in the garden.

1 First make the flower. Fold the pale yellow tissue paper sheets in half and then cut down the crease. Stack them together, giving you eight layers. Fold the orange tissue paper sheets in half and this time cut a wavy line 4in (10cm) in from each long side. Lay this centrally on top of the yellow tissue paper. Keeping all the layers together, make 1¼in (3cm) wide concertina folds all the way down the long length of the papers.

2 Tie the florist's wire around the center of the pleated tissue paper, leaving two wire tails that are 6in (15cm) long. These need to come out of the back of the flower, so make sure they are on the side that doesn't have the orange tissue showing.

3 Turn the flower over and start pulling up the orange tissue layers toward the wire in the center, two at a time. This will create the "corona" or crown of the daffodil. The outer layers will automatically open up once the central layers are pulled up.

4 Now cut three large petals into each side to make the outer section of the daffodil: use a pencil to trace three pointed petals with curved sides, using the photos as a guide. Cut around the pencil lines.

5 Pull up the tips of the petals to form a cupped shape within each petal. Tweak the central corona so that the edges overlap and form a central "bowl" and cover the central wire with the paper. You might like to glue the tissue in place here.

6 Now make the base and stem. Roll balls of air-drying modeling clay and press into the paper cup until the cup is full and the clay is compacted. Turn the cup over and push your bamboo pole through the center of the base, before the clay has time to harden. Leave for about 1 hour while the clay hardens.

7 When the clay is hard, wrap the corrugated cardboard several times around the bamboo pole to create a "stem" that is the same diameter as the base of the cup. Secure with a long piece of duct tape.

8 Tape the join between the stem and the coffee cup with more duct tape.

9 Cut the green tissue paper into long strips about 4in (10cm) wide. Use a soft paintbrush to coat the strips of paper with PVA glue and start covering the base of the cup.

10 Cover the main part of the stem in the same way, applying the strips vertically. Repeat until the whole of the stem is covered and then apply a final coat of PVA glue to the whole area.

11 When the stem has dried, use a small screwdriver or other pointed tool to make two small holes at the front of the stem and one at the back.

Create a more robust version of the stem by using chicken wire, shaped around a bamboo cane, instead of corrugated card, and filling the base with quick-dry cement rather than modeling clay.

12 Take your daffodil flower head and push the two wire tails through the two holes in the front of the stem and out through the hole at the back. Pull tightly to bring the daffodil head into place and twist to secure.

13 Cover the top of the stem with more tissue paper and PVA glue to hide the holes and twisted wire.

14 Now make the leaves. Protect your work surface with a large sheet of plastic wrap (cling film), securing it at the corners with masking tape if necessary. Pour 1 cup (250ml) PVA glue into a bowl and mix in a tablespoon of water to dilute it slightly. Lay a sheet of green tissue paper over the plastic wrap and liberally brush with the PVA glue. Work quickly and make sure you work up to the edges. Some areas can be more saturated than others—this will just add to the texture of the leaves.

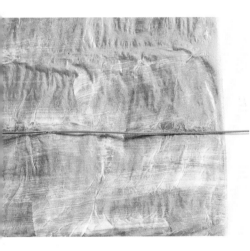

15 Quickly position a 24in (60cm) length of florist's wire on top of the tissue, about 4in (10cm) in from the edge of the paper.

16 Immediately lay your second sheet of tissue paper over the top, gently guiding it into place with your hands. The PVA should soak into this top sheet. Quickly peel the paper off the plastic wrap and hang to dry. Ideally it should hang with a droop, to create some interesting curves. Leave for about four hours. (You can use a hairdryer to speed up the process.)

17 When the paper is completely dry, use the template on page 125 to cut out daffodil leaves, making sure you position the template so that the florist's wire acts as the central leaf vein. Attach 1–2 leaves to each daffodil stem using PVA glue.

giant rose

Roses are the ultimate romantic flower and the gesture of giving a rose is symbolic of showing great love and affection. Different-colored roses also have distinct meanings: red signifies passion; pink, appreciation and admiration; white, humility and innocence. These giant roses make perfect gifts for loved ones, particularly on Mother's Day, where a beautiful giant pink rose will say "I love you" in a very special way.

1 Follow the instructions opposite to make the paper for the leaves, omitting the florist's wire. You will need to do this in advance, as the glued tissue paper needs time to dry out. Use the template on page 124 to cut out three leaves. If desired, give your leaves a jagged edging by trimming with pinking shears.

2 Use the template on page 124 to cut 15 heart-shaped petals from the crepe paper, positioning the heart template over a fold in the paper. Then create a template for teardrop-shaped petals by cutting along the dotted line on the template. Cut three teardrop-shaped petals.

3 The petals are all quite slim looking and need to be stretched. Do this by smoothing the petals over a smooth, round object or your knee to created a cupped dome shape. For larger petals use a football (make sure it is clean and dry!) or a melon. Don't stretch out the tips of the hearts at this point.

✳ ✳ ✳

You will need

(makes 1 rose, 12in (30cm) in diameter)

For the leaves

Plastic wrap (cling film)

Masking tape

Small bowl

PVA glue

Soft paintbrush

2 sheets 12 x 16in (30 x 42cm) olive green tissue paper

Template on page 124

Scissors

Pinking shears (optional)

For the rose

Template on page 124

½ x 2¾yd (2.5m) roll Italian crepe paper

Florist's tape in olive or moss green

1yd (90cm) bamboo garden cane, ¼in (5mm) in diameter

Candle

Masking tape

4 Attach your first central teardrop-shaped petal to one end of the bamboo cane by wrapping it tightly around the cane.

5 Use florist's tape to hold the petal in place. As you stretch the florist's tape and wind it around the base of the petal and top of the cane, it releases an adhesive, which bonds your petal to the bamboo cane. Apply the second and third teardrop petals, making sure that they overlap at the bottom while remaining level at the top. You should end up with something that looks like a tulip or lily.

6 Now start applying your heart-shaped petals. These should all overlap each other, so make sure when you position them that each petal covers at least half of the one applied before, so that there are no gaps in the flower. Work around the flower in the same direction until all the petals are firmly attached. If your tape breaks while you are winding and pulling, simply overlap the torn piece of tape by around ½in (1cm) with a new piece of tape and hold down firmly.

7 Attach your three green leaves using the same method as the rose petals. When you have added the final green leaf, continue winding the tape evenly down the cane. You should be able to roll the cane in your hand while pulling the tape at the same time. Roll the tape around the bottom of the cane and up again, then snip off the end of the tape.

8 To curl the petals, wrap a 1in (2.5cm) candle with masking tape and then roll the tips of the petals around the candle. Pull around and down, stretching the crepe paper as you go. Repeat for all the petals. Display in a large, tall vase or hang over a doorway using ribbons.

cone flowers centerpiece

Centerpieces aren't just for special occasions—they make a great addition to any party and can be placed on the table or hung on the wall or front door. This dahlia-like, geometric cone centerpiece is made using just simple squares of paper. It is easy to make, but you'll need to set aside some time to make it as there are around 50 cones to roll and glue. There are two sizes of cone, as this helps build up a more appealing overall shape than if all the cones are the same size. I suggest using a guillotine for this project, only because it is faster and you'll achieve much cleaner edges. You can, of course, use a ruler, set square, and good pair of scissors—or, if you are really pressed for time, buy pre-cut origami papers, usually available in different pack sizes.

✳ ✳ ✳

You will need

Several sheets of 180–250gsm paper, US letter or A4 size, in assorted colors

Scissors

Glue stick

Ruler and set square or guillotine

Thick cardstock, at least 10 x 10in (25 x 25cm)

Dinner plate, 10in (25cm) in diameter

Hot glue gun (optional)

You could use any paper for this—pages from old books, magazines, newspaper, wallpaper, or two-tone papers (particularly effective as both sides of the paper are seen).

1 Cut your sheets of colored paper into the following sizes—you will need more of the first color. Stack them in color order:
20 x 6in (15cm) squares in color 1
17 x 6in (15cm) squares in color 2
9 x 6in (15cm) squares in color 3
3–5 x 4in (10cm) squares in color 4 (for the center)
You can, of course, vary how many cones you have of each color.

2 Take a square of your first color, roll it around your finger, and secure with your glue stick. This is a little fiddly at first until your first few are completed. Use the first cone you have made as a template for the rest—that way your cones will all be the same size and shape. Complete all of your cones.

3 Draw around your dinner plate onto the thick cardstock and cut out your circle. Cover with colored paper.

4 Arrange your first layer of cones so that there is a ½in (1cm) gap between each one and the ends of the cones protrude over the edge of your base by about 2½in (7cm). Glue them in place, using either a hot glue gun or glue stick.

5 Glue down the next layer of cones in the gaps between the cones of the previous layer. This time move the cones in a little so that they are not protruding over the edge as much.

6 Repeat with the third and fourth layers, moving the cones in with each layer to create a dome effect. Glue the smaller cones in the final color as before, making sure you hide any gaps that appear at the top of the dome.

mini mirror cake bunting

These days it's all about the detail—particularly when it comes to cake decorating. Frosting and sprinkles just aren't enough! These beautiful little bunting shimmers will add a modern touch to your cake. Small and simple, yet very, very effective. I've used mirrored card here, but any patterned card will do—just make sure that whatever you use matches your carefully planned party scheme.

You will need

(to decorate a standard 8in/20cm cake)

Template on page 126

Mirrored or patterned card

Scissors

Mini hole punch (or use scissor points and a cutting mat)

16in (40cm) narrow ribbon, ⅛in (3mm) wide, or striped baker's twine

2 long wooden skewers

Washi tape (optional)

Plasticine or modeling clay

Hot glue gun (optional)

1 Use the template on page 126 to cut five or six pennant shapes from your card.

2 Make a small hole in the top two corners of each pennant, either with your mini hole punch or scissor points.

3 Thread your ribbon or twine through the holes in each pennant so that you have a string of pennants.

4 Cut your wooden skewers to 9in (22cm) and cover with washi tape, if using.

5 Place two small mounds of plasticine or modeling clay about 7in (18cm) apart and push a wooden skewer into each one.

This bunting is so simple to make—why not make a string of matching bunting to go around the base of your cake stand?

6 Wrap one end of your bunting string around the top of one of the skewers, about 1in (2.5cm) from the top, and hot glue gun it in place. Alternatively, just tie the string around the skewers. Gently lift up the other end and repeat on the second skewer.

7 Space your pennants evenly along the string and trim off any excess ribbon or twine if required. Situating them closer together will give the bunting line a deeper curve or swag. Maybe experiment before you decide exactly where you want these to go, otherwise your cake will have a few unwanted holes appearing! Then when your cake is ready, simply insert the mini bunting poles in place.

giant gerbera

Giant flowers are always a talking point and this gerbera will be the envy of your guests! The gerbera is currently the fifth most popular flower in the world behind the rose, carnations, chrysanthemums, and tulips. With their bold colors, gerberas seem to convey cheerfulness and these giant versions would look great outdoors, lining the path to a party tent or barbecue area. They can simply be staked into the ground—we used a 3ft (1m) slim bamboo pole, but you could always use a longer length than this.

✳ ✳ ✳

You will need

(makes 1 flower)

4 sheets 20 x 30in (50 x 75cm) tissue paper in one color for main flower petals

Scissors

4 sheets 20 x 30in (50 x 75cm) tissue paper in contrast color for flower center

Ruler

2 sheets 20 x 30in (50 x 75cm) tissue paper in green for the flower underside

Florist's wire

Narrow bamboo pole or plant support stick

Green florist's tape

1 Fold the four sheets of tissue paper for the main flower petals in half along the shorter length, make a sharp crease, and cut along the fold to create eight sheets of paper that are 20 x 15in (50 x 38cm).

2 Repeat with the contrasting sheets of tissue (for the center), but this time measure, fold, and crease 6 in (15cm) in from one edge and cut along this crease. You should be left with a stack of eight sheets, 9 x 20in (23 x 50cm).

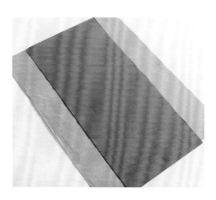

3 Stack your main color sheets into a neat pile and place your contrasting paper centrally on top.

4 Repeat step 2 with the two sheets of green tissue to create four sheets that are 9 x 20in (23 x 50cm). Fold ⅝in (1.5cm) concertina folds along the length of the green tissue and then cut long diagonal cuts on either side at the tips to create long, leaflike shapes.

5 Unravel the folds and lay this stack of green tissue paper on the table. Place the stack of colored sheets on top—you should now have a "sandwich" with the contrast (flower center) color on top, the main color in the middle, and the leaves on the bottom.

6 You need to try to keep all of the paper stacked together, so hold all of the sheets very firmly. They will move slightly, but this will just add to the texture. Make your first concertina fold about ¾in (2cm) deep, then turn the stack of paper over and fold it again. Keep creating concertina folds until all of your paper is folded in a very tight bundle.

7 Tie a piece of florist's wire around the center of the folded tissue, leaving two tails about 4in (10cm) long at the back of the flower (leaf side).

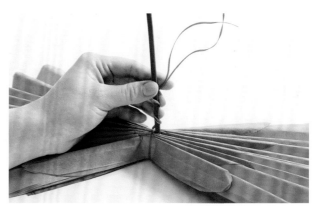

8 Make long diagonal snips down one side of each fold of the main flower and then round off each cut. We will come back to cutting the longer petals once the next step is complete.

9 Take the bamboo pole or stick and find the most central part of the back of the flower where you can insert the stick as far as it will go. Because the layers of paper are folded so tightly, the pole will hold quite firmly. Wrap the wire tails around the bamboo pole and secure tightly with the florist's tape.

10 Then carefully start teasing out and pulling your leaf shape petals out toward the pole. Once you have two layers pulled out, wrap these around the pole and secure in place with more florist's tape.

11 Continue wrapping the florist's tape in a diagonal, evenly spaced spiral down to the base of the pole.

12 Gently pull out the layers of paper in the middle of the flower so that they form a 6in (15cm) center. Pulling out these layers will cause the outer petals to open out, too.

13 Use scissors to trim off the central part of the flower so that the inner petals are approximately ¾–1in (2–3cm) high. Finally, make long, straight cuts down the creases of the large petals to give the gerbera petals their unique look.

tissue bauble heart

The idea for these molded tissue "baubles" came about some years ago when I was faced with a deadline for a client: make 1000 mini poms to decorate a sign in two days. I realized that by pressing tissue paper into a small glass votive (tea light) holder, between us we could easily press out about 100 poms per hour. These baubles really remind me of those mini macarons that you see in fabulous cake shops in pretty colors.

You will need

Several sheets of tissue paper in 2 colors

Scissors

Mold for bauble—votive (tea light) holder, egg cup, small glass pot

Template on page 119

20 x 20in (50 x 50cm) square of thick cardstock or corrugated card

Craft knife (optional)

Glue gun

1 If you are using large sheets of tissue paper, cut them in half. You will need about 30 pieces of tissue paper in each color, approximately 20 x 15in (50 x 38cm).

2 Take a sheet of tissue paper and use your hands to scrunch it up into a small ball, leaving one corner of the sheet unscrunched.

3 Push the ball into the mold to get a nice round shape, then take it out and wrap the unscrunched paper neatly around the ball. Push back into the mold as firmly as you can and hold it there for a few moments.

4 When you remove the bauble from the mold, you will find it puffs out a little—this is fine. Repeat to make 30 baubles in each color (to cover the heart).

5 Use the template on page 119 to cut out a heart shape from the card, using scissors or a craft knife. I like the natural color of the card showing through, but you can of course paint or cover the card in paper first. Use a hot glue gun to stick the baubles to the card, starting with the outer edge of the heart.

6 Continue adding baubles, alternating your two colors as you go. (Another idea would be to use a selection of colors, graduating from dark to light.) Repeat until the surface of the card is fully covered. You may want to lay all your baubles out in position before glueing to make sure they fit.

waxed floating lilies

If you have a pond, these pretty floating flowers will liven up your setting for an outdoor party. However, they would look equally stunning indoors floating in a large glass bowl. They are made using waxed tissue paper—look for double-coated paper, as it will give better results. These exotic floating flowers need only a very small amount of paper to stay afloat!

You will need

(makes two flowers)

1 sheet green double-coated waxed tissue paper, 20 x 30in (50 x 75cm)

1 sheet pink/yellow/white double-coated waxed tissue paper, 20 x 30in (50 x 75cm)

4in (10cm) plastic-coated garden wire for each flower

Scissors

Water-resistant LED lights (optional)

Try this

Place water-resistant LED votives (tea lights) in the center of the flowers to create a very beautiful lighting system. Imagine a whole pond full of them…

1 Fold the green tissue paper into quarters and then cut along the creases to create four sheets of paper. Repeat with your colored paper. Lay two sheets of colored tissue on top of two sheets of green tissue and start making concertina folds, approximately 1–1¼in (2.5–3cm) wide, all the way down the long length of the paper.

2 Secure the folded tissue in the middle with a piece of garden wire—simply twist the wire where it meets the paper.

3 Now cut long curves into both ends of the folded paper.

4 Hold your flower with the green paper facing downward. Lift up the first layer of colored tissue, but don't pull it all the way to the center; leave 1in (2.5cm) between the wire and the upward-pointing petal. Repeat with the second layer and work your way around the flower.

5 Curl the tips of the green layer upward; this will prevent water from tumbling over the sides and weighing down the flower. Repeat with the remaining sheets of green and colored tissue paper to make a second floating lily.

tea light votive covers

The perfectly neat geometric cuts in this delicate yet simple project make the votive look modern and fresh. The light shines through the openings and casts wonderful shadows on the surroundings. To cover a vase, you could use the same patterns scaled up to a larger size or repeated over a bigger sheet of paper.

You will need

(makes 1 votive cover)

Glass tea light holder or small jam jar

Soft tape measure

1 sheet of vellum or ordinary paper (between 180 and 250gsm)

Scissors

Template on page 127

Black marker pen

Masking tape

Light box (or window)

Fine retractable pencil

Craft knife

Cutting mat

Soft eraser

Magic tape

1 First work out what size your tea light cover needs to be. Measure the height of your tea light holder/glass jar, using a soft tape measure. Now measure the circumference and add ¾in (2cm) to this measurement to allow for wrap-around. Cut a rectangle of your chosen paper to these measurements—you should be able to wrap it around your tea light holder, completely covering it.

2 Photocopy the template on page 127 and go over the lines on the photocopy with a thick black pen. This will be the template you will trace the shapes from onto your rectangle of paper. (You can use this template multiple times.)

3 Place your rectangle of paper on top of the template and secure it in place with masking tape, either on a light box or on a window. Trace over the lines from one row with a light fine pencil. You can then trace the other two rows of shapes or you can move the template if you'd like more or less space between the rows of shapes.

4 When you've finished tracing the shapes remove the template, place the paper on a cutting mat, and cut the lines with your craft knife. Use your eraser to rub out any visible pencil lines. Rub in the direction of the cut, not against it.

5 Turn the paper over, roll it around your tea light cover or jar, and secure it in place with magic tape. When it's in place, gently lift up the tips of the shapes so that they are raised a little but not fully. They shouldn't be opened back more than halfway.

Be careful

Never leave a candle unattended. Alternatively, use LED tea lights.

geo box display

These look great when hung with paper poms and tassels; their geometric lines break up the softness of the petals and fringes. They can be hung vertically or draped horizontally, but could also be incorporated into a mobile— for example, instead of the stars in the 3-D Star Mobile (see page 39).

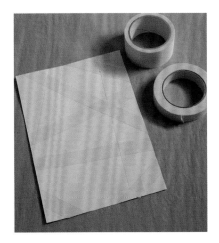

1 Take a sheet of card or paper and stick down lengths of masking tape in lines that criss-cross at random angles. Do this on all of your sheets.

2 Decide what colors you want to use and paint your card or paper, painting over the masking tape. Cover the entire sheet and choose different-colored stripes or swirly patterns. Do not dilute the paint with water, but try not to over-saturate the card as this will cause it to warp and ripple. Repeat for all the sheets and leave to dry.

3 When the painted sheets are completely dry, carefully peel off the masking tape to reveal your pattern.

You will need

(makes 16 geo shapes)

8 sheets of thick paper or thin cardstock (320gsm)

Masking tape

Acrylic paint in bright colors (use neon or glow-in-the-dark paints for extra zing)

Paintbrush

Template on page 126

Sharp pencil

Metal ruler

Craft knife and cutting mat

Scoring tool, such as a bone folder (optional)

3¼yd (3m) butcher's twine or narrow ribbon, ¼in (5mm) wide

Clear all-purpose glue or hot glue gun

Glitter (optional)

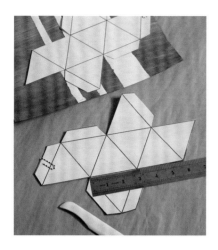  

4 Use the template on page 126 to create a "net" for your shapes. Use a metal ruler to draw around this on your painted card, then cut around the lines using a craft knife and cutting mat. Use a scoring tool or sharp pencil to score along the fold lines.

5 Fold along the scored lines to create your shape. Fold the tabs inward, but do not glue them yet.

6 To hang as a horizontal garland, make two small holes at the top of one of the points of your shape, using a sharp pencil or the point of a pair of scissors. Do this on all your shapes. Start threading the butcher's twine or ribbon through the holes you have made in each shape, then use clear all-purpose glue or a hot glue gun to glue all the tabs. Hold for a few seconds to allow the glue to set. Repeat for all 16 shapes.

Try this

To hang as a vertical garland, make small holes at the top and bottom of each shape once they have been glued together. Thread the boxes onto lengths of narrow ribbon—to make this easier, tape the end of a piece of ribbon to a wooden skewer and push the skewer through the boxes. When you are happy with the positioning of each box on the ribbon, glue in place with a hot glue gun.

blossoms on a branch

This is a lovely installation piece that can be left up all year round. It is a luxury to have real flowers in your home every week and it's always a shame to see them wilt in the vase, knowing that in a few days they will be put on the compost heap or organic recycling bin. Our blossom poms bring a found tree branch back to life—and it won't need tending to! Each blossom has tiny petals cut into the tissue paper, but if you find this step too fiddly you can leave the petals uncut—the end result will still be just as pretty.

❋ ❋ ❋

You will need

Tree branch (see page 111)

Nailbrush

Lint-free muslin cloth

Sponge

Petroleum jelly

Baby oil

Soft paintbrush

Pruning secateurs

Brown 32-gauge florist's wire

Wire cutters

1 sheet 30 x 20in (75 x 50cm) tissue paper (this will make 16 blossoms)

Scissors

Wooden toothpick or tweezers

1 Scrub your branch clean with a nailbrush and then dry by hand with a lint-free muslin cloth. To give your branch a lovely glossy appearance, use a sponge to apply petroleum jelly to the branch and then the following day brush it with baby oil using a soft paintbrush. Your branch will smell lovely. (Your hands will feel soft, too!) Decide how dense or sparse you would like the blossom branch to look. Prune any unwanted branches as desired. Clip these as close to the main stalk as possible, so that you achieve a neat look. The best stumps can be touched up with brown paint to match the branch or simply add a small blossom to disguise it.

2 Cut 16 pieces of florist's wire, each 4¾in (12cm) long, and bend each one in half. Set to one side. Take your sheet of tissue paper and fold it in half three times so you have a rectangle that is eight layers deep. Now fold this in half four times, creasing firmly each time. Open out the last four folds—you should have a grid of 16 rectangles on your eight-layer sheet. Holding the paper firmly, use scissors to cut the tissue paper into 16 stacks of tissue paper, following the lines on your grid.

3 Take one of the small stacks of paper and fold over ⅛in (3mm) at one end. Continue making concertina folds until you get to the end. Take one of your pieces of wire and place the center point of your folded paper in the bend of the wire. Pinch the wire between your thumb and forefinger and twist three times to secure the wire over the folded tissue paper.

4 Fan out the folds of your pom and with the tip of your scissors, make a small ¼in (5mm) cut in the center fold. Repeat on the opposite side. Close the folds back again. Holding the first half of one side (that you have just snipped into), cut a small petal shape into the ends. Repeat on all four sections.

5 To fluff the poms, hold the wire stem tightly and open out the mini pom into a fan shape. Use tweezers or a wooden toothpick to tease out the flat layer that is facing you. Carefully pull this as far as you can toward the center of the pom. Repeat on the other side. Tease and fluff up the remaining layers.

6 To attach the blossoms to the branches, simply wrap the wire around the branch and twist the ends to secure. Continue until you have attached all of your poms. If you feel it needs more blossoms, then make up as many as you need.

Choosing the right branch

Decide if you will be hanging your branch on a wall or resting it on a shelf, as this will dictate what shape of branch you need to source. Bear in mind that you can always trim and cut a branch to suit. If you are sitting the finished piece on a shelf, then you'll probably need a slim, non-bushy branch so that it has room to lean back against the wall. If you are hanging it on a wall, you can use a more elaborate and busy-looking branch.

Do be aware of any restrictions about taking branches from public spaces and parks—contact your local parks department for permission if necessary.

paper wisteria

The wistful, lightweight, and thoroughly delicate flower wisteria is a quintessentially English country-garden climber which, sadly, only flowers for a few months of the year in April until May or early June. I have long tried to find a way to capture this delicate flower and think that this simple line of crepe paper twists does the trick!

You will need

1 x 40ft (12m) roll of 2in (5cm) crepe paper streamers in lilac, white, or pink

1 x 40ft (12m) roll of 2in (5cm) crepe paper streamers in pale green

30in (75cm) paper-covered wire or florist's wire

Scissors

Hot glue gun

1 Cut the following lengths of colored crepe paper streamer for each "bunch" of wisteria: 1 x 25in (62.5cm), 2 x 20in (50cm), 1 x 16in (40cm), and 1 x 12in (30cm). Cut 1 x 20in (50cm) and 1 x 12in (30cm) length from the green crepe paper streamer. Cut a 16in (40cm) length of paper-covered wire or florist's wire.

2 Take one of the cut streamers and, holding the end flat over your thumb, twist the loose tail once until it is facing the same way as your first twist. Repeat this action all the way to the end of the streamer. You are making a series of little thumb-sized "cups." Repeat for the other lengths, including the green ones.

3 Take a few twisted streamers and find the mid-point of each piece. Position them near the end of your wire, making sure the green lengths will be underneath the colored lengths when they're hung up. Twist the wire around the streamers to secure them in place. You'll be left with a lovely cascade of colored lengths with your green underneath.

4 Repeat step 3 until you have the required amount of bunches. You can either hang them separately, as we have done, or hang them all together in a large bunch.

5 If the "twisteria" is protruding out at odd-looking angles, simply apply a damp sponge to the piece or pieces at the glued end of the cluster and flatten down or manipulate to suit. You can trim the end of any lengths by tearing or cutting with scissors.

coffee-filter wreath

Coffee filters have a lovely soft texture to them, while still being robust and very flexible. And, being filters, they are very absorbent, which helps when dyeing them with your own colors. I've kept the color palette a light mix of neutrals and pale pinks, with a few greens for the leaves. This project has to be made in several stages that each need a few hours. The dyed filters need a drying time of around four hours, as does the wreath base.

1 Prepare your five dyes: light pink, dark pink, orange, brown, and green. For the two pink dyes, orange, and green, add a few drops of food coloring to a small bowl of water—add more drops for the darker pink. For the brown dye, add two or three tea bags to a small bowl of boiling water. Let cool and remove the tea bags before using.

2 Set aside the 10 bleached filters, then divide up the rest into 70 for pink, 40 for neutrals, and 10 for greens. Wearing rubber gloves to protect your hands, dip your filters into your mixes so that they are submerged and will absorb the colors. Wring them out and then peg them onto a line or lay them over radiators to dry. This will take a few hours.

✳ ✳ ✳

You will need

Several packs of coffee filters, 6–8in (15–20cm) in diameter—you'll need at least 130, including 10 bleached (white) filters

Food coloring in pink, orange, and green

Tea bags

5 bowls or pots for mixing dyes

Rubber gloves

4-ft (1.2-m) length of foam pipe insulation (available at any hardware store)

Scissors

Duct tape

Several sheets of neutral tissue paper

PVA glue

Masking tape

Stapler

Hot glue gun

Template on page 126

3 In the meantime, the wreath base can be made. Use scissors to cut two rectangles of foam away from one end of the pipe. Cut corresponding pieces from the other end, so that the two ends will fit together in a sort of dovetail joint. Place the two ends of the pipe together and tape securely with duct tape. You will now have a lovely round wreath base.

4 Tear up enough strips of tissue paper to completely cover the wreath base and paste to the wreath base using PVA glue. Allow to dry—this could take up to four hours, but you can speed up the process with a hairdryer.

5 When your filters are dry, start making the ruffled flowers: Stack five filters on top of each other (three dark and two light), and then fold them into quarters.

6 Use scissors to cut scalloped or pointed petals into the ends. Staple the fold at the base to secure.

7 Holding the stapled end, open out the layers—but as you do this, pinch and twist the base of the flower; this will create a very pretty ruffled flower. When all the layers are fluffed out, tape the base of the flower with masking tape to hold it in place until it is glued to the wreath. Repeat to create nine flowers like this, using a mix of pink, brown, and white filters.

8 To make the taped flower: Make a stack of three filters (use graduated colors or a mix) and fold into quarters. Cut a scalloped edge along the top and then cut out the center, again with a scalloped edge. Set the outer pieces aside to use in step 9. Repeat to make about 20–30 flower centers, depending on how full you want your wreath to look.

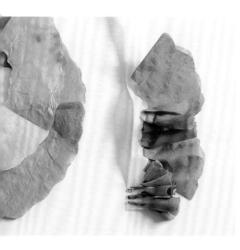

9 Twist each flower center piece at the base to create a petal and press two or three of these onto a strip of masking tape about 10in (25cm) long. Then take the reserved outer pieces and almost pleat these as you stick them down, creating a long ruffle on the tape.

10 Take your ruffled strip and start to roll the tape, starting where the center petals are. This will create a very pretty but shallow ruffled rose.

11 Repeat to make 10–15 of these flowers.

Attach fake berries and fruit to the wreath for a spring or summer display, or icy blue and silver berries and leaves for a winter look.

12 To make the leaves, use the template on page 126 to cut six or seven spiky leaf shapes from each green filter. These leaves will be glued into your wreath while you are attaching the flowers to the base.

13 Now start attaching your flowers—a hot glue gun is essential here. Think about how you would like the composition to look; you could cluster the larger flowers together to create an asymmetric display or go haphazard and boho and literally "pick and stick"! Use the smaller flowers around the larger ones and fill in the gaps with the leaves.

templates

Here are all the templates you'll need for the projects in this book. Actual-size templates can be traced off the page. Half-size and quarter-size templates have been reduced to fit on the page and will need to be enlarged on a photocopier by the given percentage.

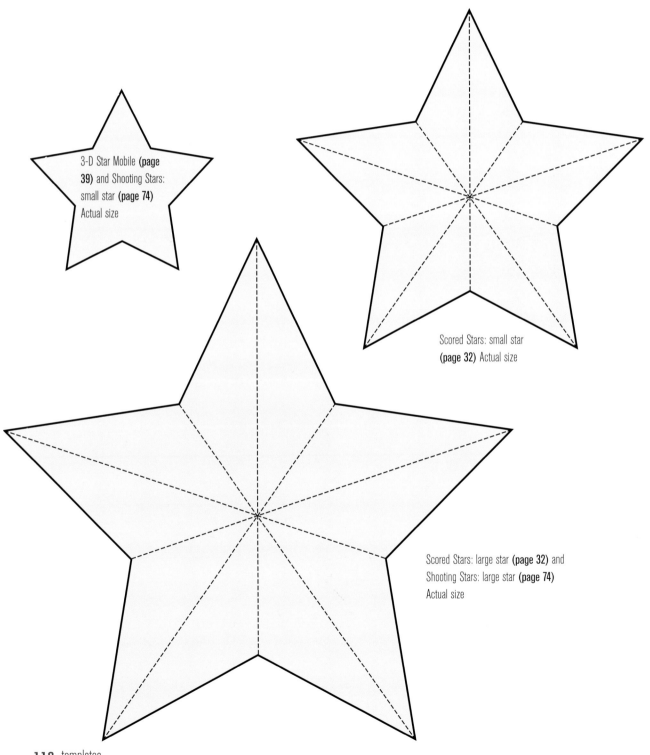

3-D Star Mobile (page 39) and Shooting Stars: small star (page 74) Actual size

Scored Stars: small star (page 32) Actual size

Scored Stars: large star (page 32) and Shooting Stars: large star (page 74) Actual size

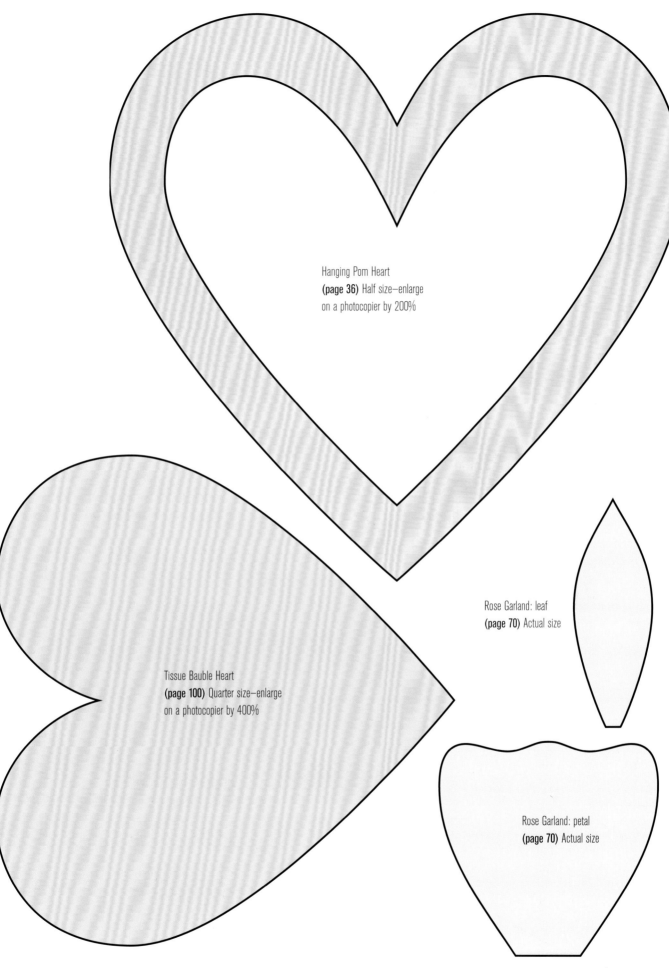

Hanging Pom Heart
(page 36) Half size—enlarge
on a photocopier by 200%

Tissue Bauble Heart
(page 100) Quarter size—enlarge
on a photocopier by 400%

Rose Garland: leaf
(page 70) Actual size

Rose Garland: petal
(page 70) Actual size

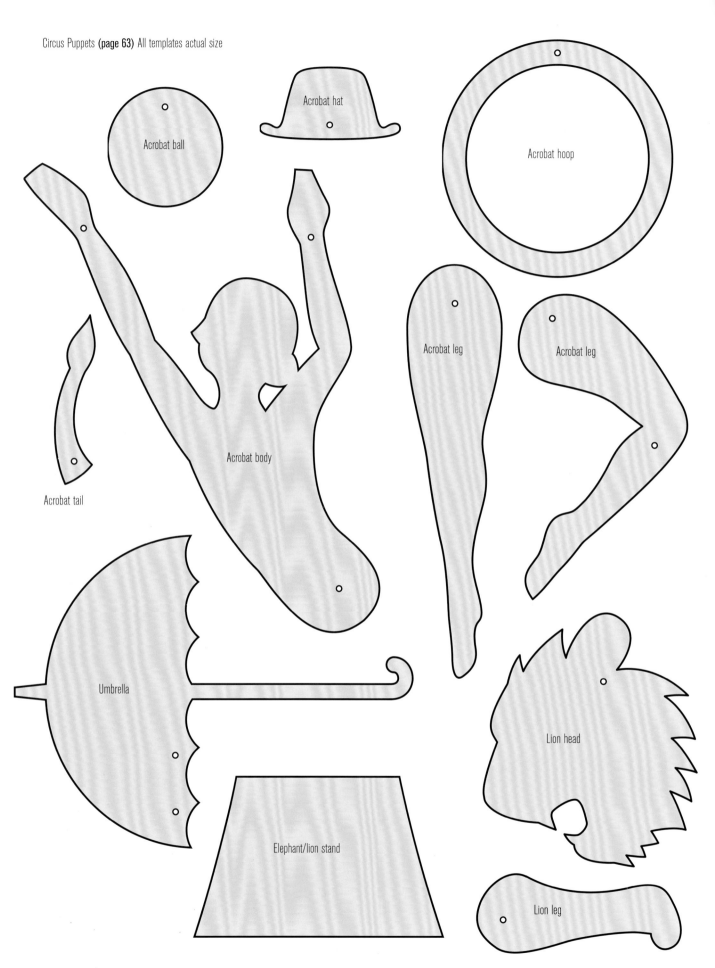

Acrobat ball

Acrobat hat

Acrobat hoop

Acrobat tail

Acrobat body

Acrobat leg

Acrobat leg

Umbrella

Lion head

Elephant/lion stand

Lion leg

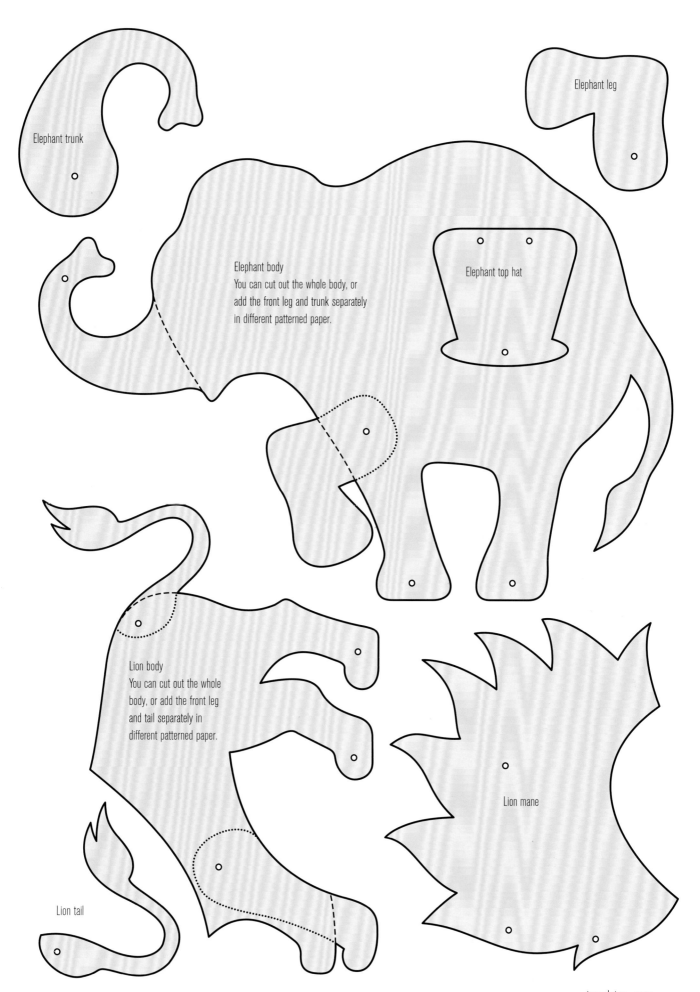

Elephant trunk

Elephant leg

Elephant body
You can cut out the whole body, or
add the front leg and trunk separately
in different patterned paper.

Elephant top hat

Lion body
You can cut out the whole
body, or add the front leg
and tail separately in
different patterned paper.

Lion mane

Lion tail

Top Hat Piñata: brim
(page 42) Half size—enlarge on
a photocopier by 200%
NB: You might find it easiest to cut out
the inner circle (indicated by the dotted
line) before cutting out the triangles.

Mini Pom Cake Toppers
(page 23) Actual size

Leaves on Twine
(page 48) Actual size

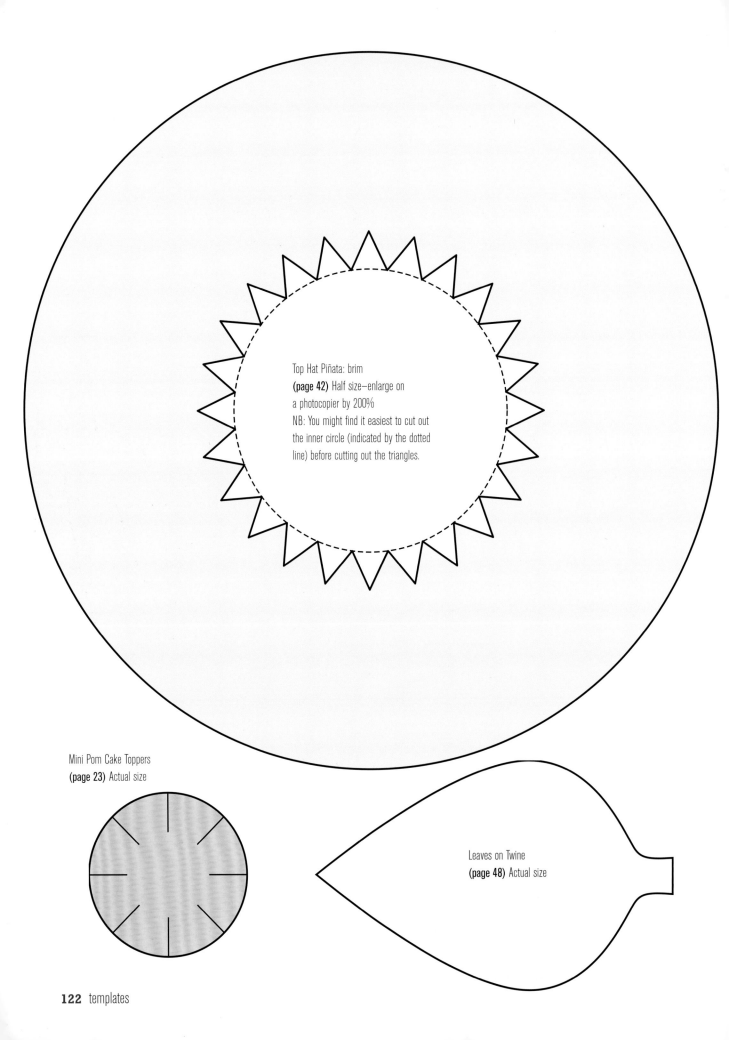

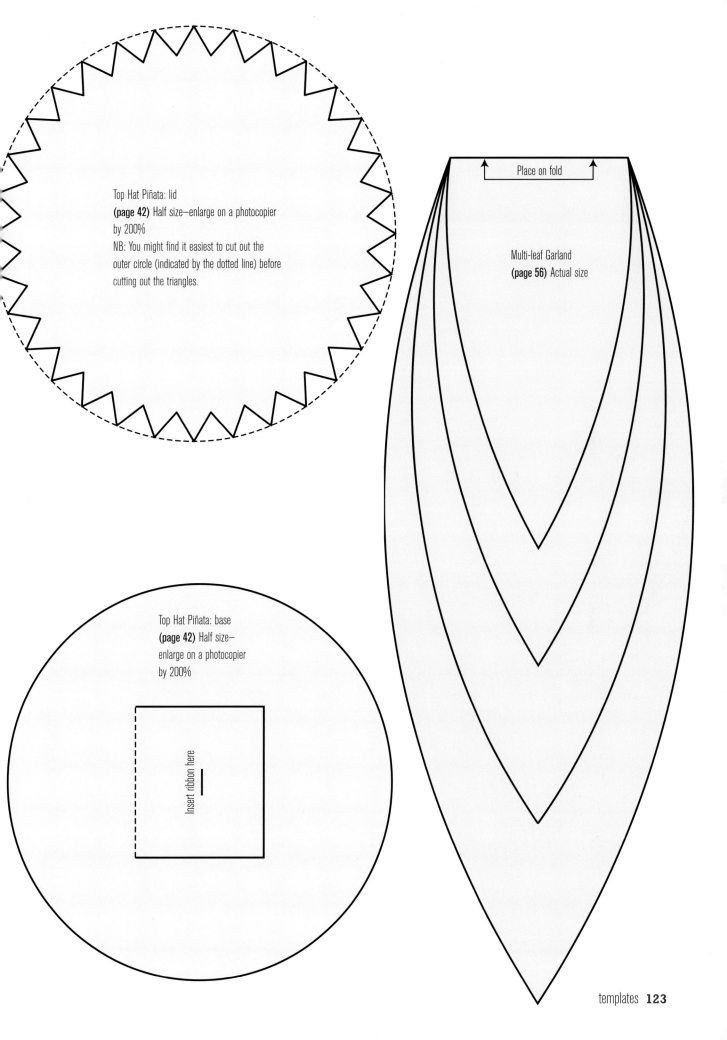

Top Hat Piñata: lid
(page 42) Half size—enlarge on a photocopier by 200%
NB: You might find it easiest to cut out the outer circle (indicated by the dotted line) before cutting out the triangles.

Place on fold

Multi-leaf Garland
(page 56) Actual size

Top Hat Piñata: base
(page 42) Half size—enlarge on a photocopier by 200%

Insert ribbon here

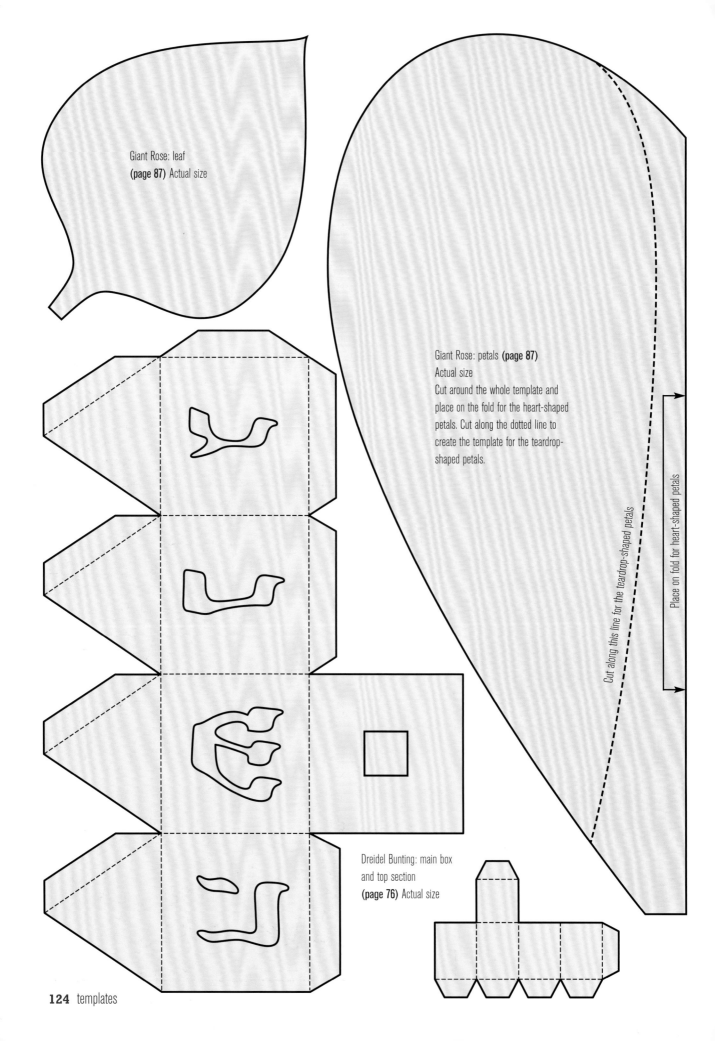

Giant Rose: leaf
(page 87) Actual size

Giant Rose: petals **(page 87)**
Actual size
Cut around the whole template and
place on the fold for the heart-shaped
petals. Cut along the dotted line to
create the template for the teardrop-
shaped petals.

Cut along this line for the teardrop-shaped petals

Place on fold for heart-shaped petals

Dreidel Bunting: main box
and top section
(page 76) Actual size

Giant Daffodils: leaf
(page 82) Actual size

Papel Picado **(page 60)**
Actual size

Place on fold

Place on fold

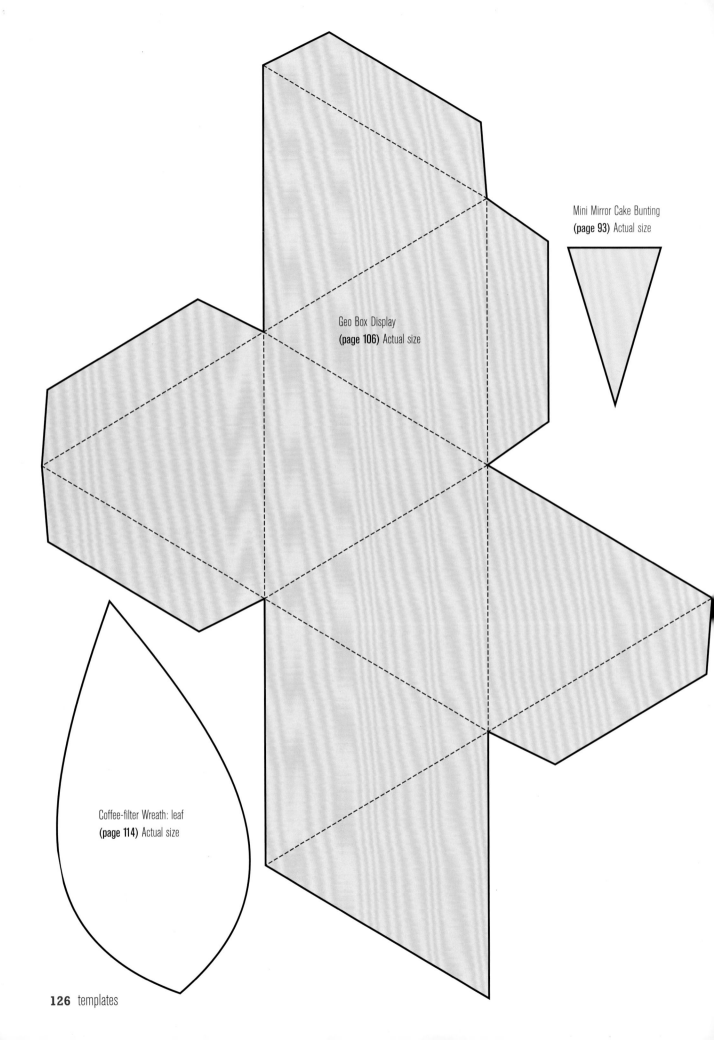

Mini Mirror Cake Bunting
(page 93) Actual size

Geo Box Display
(page 106) Actual size

Coffee-filter Wreath: leaf
(page 114) Actual size

suppliers

Author's website
www.paperpoms.co.uk

US and Canada
Tissue paper, crepe paper, and paper streamers
www.cartefini.com
(for Italian crepe paper)
www.favors.com
(for crepe paper streamers)
www.partyvalue.com (for Mylar foil)
www.seamanpaper.com
(for SatinWrap premium quality tissue)
www.wrapturetissue.com

Scissors and shears
www.germanysolingen.com

Plant canes and garden wire
www.gardencentreguide.com
www.homedepot.com

Decorative masking tape
www.mt-tape.us

General craft and papercraft supplies
www.acmoore.com
www.artsuppliesonline.com
www.hobbylobby.com
www.michaels.com
www.paper-source.com

Other useful websites
www.amazon.com
www.ebay.com
www.marthastewart.com
www.molliemakes.com
www.pinterest.com

UK
Tissue paper, crepe paper, and paper streamers
www.paperchase.co.uk
www.wrappingranch.co.uk

Scissors and rotary cutters
www.fiskars.co.uk

General stationery supplies, including hole punches
www.staples.co.uk

Decorative masking tape
www.lovelytape.co.uk
www.paperchase.co.uk

Plant canes, garden wire, and floristry supplies
www.diy.com
www.homebase.co.uk
www.oasisfloral.co.uk

Paper-covered wire
www.therange.co.uk

Ribbon
www.berisfords-ribbons.co.uk
www.johnlewis.com
www.vvrouleaux.com

General craft and papercraft supplies
www.craftcreations.com
www.hobbycraft.co.uk
www.papercraft4you.co.uk
www.thepapercraftcompany.co.uk
www.totalpapercraft.co.uk

Other useful websites
www.amazon.co.uk
www.ebay.co.uk
www.kirstieallsopp.co.uk
www.molliemakes.com
www.pinterest.com

Tea Light Votive Cover
(page 104) Actual size

index

acknowledgments

My thanks go to: **CICO Books**, for their guidance and free rein on the designs and projects within the book; **Eleanor Hutchinson** for her great organizational and crafting skills and her creative input for the book, and for seamlessly running my studio while I've been busy being a mum; **Molly Syrett** for helping us make and create some of the projects in the book; **Laela Bernard** for her exquisite crafting skills and who made some of the wonderful makes in the book; **Jessica Knight** for stepping in at the last moment to make the final projects; **Mr P**, for all of his immaculate pom folding and cheery advice over the years.

Thanks also to: my "Fairy Pom Mother" **Sue Bodinetz**, who has encouraged me to persist with the poms but also to diversify from the get-go—an amazing mentor with impeccable taste; **Bea**, for her hard work and support from the start of Paperpoms in 2009; **Linda Davis** for her much-needed wisdom and advice before the start of the book; **Tabitha Rout** at Circus Brixton for the loan of some superb vintage props from her eclectic retro lifestyle shop in Brixton Village; **Kevin Rimmington** and **Philip Vian** at Rimmington Vian, who gave me my first job after art school and who taught me how to run a creative studio; **Johnny Grey** at Johnny Grey studios, who took me on after my degree and brought out the project manager and the interior designer in me; **Ann Lyndsey**, my first art teacher, who encouraged me to express myself through painting and who believed in me; **Julia Heynat**, for her great guidance on how to merge my personality with my business.

Plus, to all my family and friends who have put up with my never-ending work commitments and who are always cheering me on, in particular: my mother, **Maggie Carr**, for her never-ending patience, unconditional love, and support, and for looking after baby Jasper while I wrote this book; my fiancé, **Clive Jackson**, for all of his sound advice and for steering me in the right direction; my sister, **Christina Carr**, for her love, enthusiasm, and support and for always being on my side!

And thank you to all of my clients and customers who have embraced the handmade craft movement and helped me take my company to where it is now.